THE ADVENTURE

A Memoir in Spirituality and Schizophrenia

Lynn Johnson

authorHOUSE®

AuthorHouse™
1663 Liberty Drive
Bloomington, IN 47403
www.authorhouse.com
Phone: 1-800-839-8640

First published by AuthorHouse   12/14/2009

ISBN: 978-1-4490-5249-2 (e)
ISBN: 978-1-4490-5248-5 (sc)

Library of Congress Control Number: 2009912335

Printed in the United States of America
Bloomington, Indiana

This book is printed on acid-free paper.

This book is dedicated to Gavyn, who has always been there for me. It is also for my family and friends who have helped me through this illness and accompanied me on my spiritual journey. I thank Tyrtle for her shamanic healing and help in editing and the production of the book. I thank those who have provided me with encouragement in writing the book and feedback about changes in the book. I thank Linda, George, Aminah, and Tara for their wisdom, respect and caring. I also thank those in my meditation groups, Paint Branch Unitarian Universalist Church, yoga classes, acupressure exchanges, sacred circle dancing groups, and drum circles for providing accepting communities.

CONTENTS

INTRODUCTION

Vulnerability
3/2/08

Sinking back
into
the wild woman
escape artist
reliving moments
or days
or lives
questioning
who is in
the driver's seat
questioning
how and why
and wherefore
my anniversary
of one year
locked in and out
in split worlds
which reality
is real
stable enough
to know all perception
lies
as do many thoughts
and beliefs
writing
so that others may enter
and I may see from afar
the distance walked

I write "so that others may enter and I may see from afar the distance walked." So that I may see the distance crawled, the monsters faced, the split realities that have formed my world. I fear that by recreating the abyss I might once more fall into it. Fall out of my "normalcy" into an uncontrollable world directed by an unknown part of me. Isn't that a fear that we all have? It's just that my fears, my travel, my states are extreme and labeled psychotic, part of my "schizo-affective disorder."[1]

Five times in five years I have suffered psychotic episodes and have been hospitalized as a result: May 3-6, and October 1-6, 2003, at Washington Adventist Hospital; September 7, 2004, at Holy Cross Hospital; September 8-20, 2004, at Washington Adventist; October 19, 2004, at North Arundel Hospital; October 20-November 4, 2004, at Sheppard and Enoch Pratt Hospital; and March 9-20, 2007, at Montgomery General Hospital. It was only after the fourth time, my stay at Sheppard Pratt, that I realized I have a "mental illness." The explanation for why I have a mental illness that I like best is a chemical imbalance or hormonal imbalance. Yet no one has found these nor is looking for them, at least in my case.

I have tried a number of complementary health practices including clinical and process acupressure, jin shin jytsu, shiatsu, yoga, and shamanic rituals and journeying. I have also explored Buddhist psychology and have a daily meditation practice. It is difficult to know what has helped and how much it has helped, but I believe that these treatments have built my inner resources so that between psychotic breaks I have assumed an air of 'normalcy.'

It seems that the proper allopathic medicine and lack of stress also protect me from ongoing psychosis, but the line is thin, and it is hard to avoid psychotic breaks when the cause is unknown. All of the anti-psychotic medications have side effects including a predisposition to diabetes, weight gain, and tardive dyskenesia (trembling with Parkinsonism symptoms).

It is almost impossible to realize that I can create my own world of fear where people or extraterrestrials are chasing me in order to kill me. In this world of fear, I believe fully that my loved ones are dead or will be killed by the same forces that are after me. In these realities, I see and feel global catastrophes and am sure they will happen. How do I account for these thoughts that lead to extremist beliefs and then the actions that are based on these beliefs? My "talk therapy" has not revealed the origin of these thoughts. Perhaps these words may shed some light on my illness and the complex thoughts and behavior that are driven by such illness.

Although I realize that I have a mental illness, I am not mentally ill. I am much larger than my illness and choose not to be defined solely by it. I am incredibly fortunate to not have had this illness until the age of 53 and to have my family and friends accept it in a supportive way. My schizo-affective disorder has taught me a number of things: 1) question my thoughts and beliefs; 2) trust in my body because it won't lie to me like my mind does; 3) be compassionate to everyone I meet, because we all have our stories; 4) live in the present moment, letting go of the past and the future; and 5) wake up to the beauty and fragility of our natural world.

As part of the illness, I have trouble with my memory and can no longer remember telephone numbers or work with figures beyond balancing my check book. I have changed most of the names of people in this book. My poetry that is included was written on the date given below the title of the poem. I find that it often expresses a feeling state that I can not put into prose. Some of the times, places, and events may not be facts of the external world, but what I write is as close as I can come to accurately reporting what I experienced.

This book is written for my family and friends. It is also written for those who suffer a mental illness and their family and friends, health care workers, counselors, social workers, psychiatrists, and general public who may be looking for a deeper understanding of mental illness. I interweave my spiritual journey through my psychotic episodes for I believe that mind, body, spirit, and emotions are conjoined and can not be separated from one another.

STEPPED OFF

6/29/03

Stepped
off
the whirring
hamster wheel
of busyness
before the thousand foot drop
I hung
suspended
weightless
shivering
ever cooler
as I leave my shell behind
metamorphosis
cutting through
layers of reality
as a bow through waves
rocky
butt hitting hard
jolting and compacting
vertebrae pressure
then turning
to ride the wave
opening
streaming
white gold
coursing
through
up and down
me

I have lived a full and healthy life. However, after 33 years of working professionally, raising two children, being in two marriages and one committed partnership, I found myself locked in a mental ward in Washington Adventist Hospital. At the time I believed that I and all of the creatures of the earth were suffering from radioactive poisoning through the water and soil. I felt that, by going to the hospital, the doctors would discover this radioactive poisoning and at least document it. Instead I was admitted to the psychiatric ward on May 1, 2003. . I viewed this as an adventure, another step in my own spiritual growth. By spirituality I mean my relationship with the Universe (God, Allah, Tao, Light field of love, Source -all different names for the same thing) and my relationship with all beings and the interdependent web of life around me.

Numerous events led up to my hospitalization, including a kidney operation three months prior. In December 2002 after nine years, I lost my position at a prestigious non-profit organization due to a reorganization. I also ended my business partnership of nine months and my consultancy company. I had wanted to spread my wings and fly as a small business owner, but I felt like I was crashing back to earth. I decided to go back into research administration, a profession that I had been in for 16 years. I also decided to devote myself more to my current life partner, even though I felt stifled in the relationship. I said to the Universe that, if it had other plans for me, I was ready for them. Within a week of saying that prayer, I was diagnosed with a tumor the size of a grapefruit on my kidney! I was shocked and distressed when I was told that without surgery there was a 25% chance of the tumor rupturing and killing me. I did not want to undergo surgery but decided to do so.

I used the time between the first week of December and February 6, the date of the surgery, to try many complementary medicine techniques and energy work in the hope that the tumor would significantly disappear. I didn't have them take another MRI to see if it was getting smaller, I just went with western medical advice. I spent a goodly portion of my time adopting a positive outlook and analyzing what was really important to me. There is nothing like the presence of death to help one gain some clarity on life. I chose to view what was happening to me as an adventure! I felt the love of so many people before, during, and after the operation. If I had died then, it would have been okay. After the surgery, pain altered my blissful state as it became a constant companion for six weeks after the surgery. Some discomfort continues to today, more than six years later.

At the end of six weeks, I moved out of our house and separated from my partner of 13 years. I and my son took up residence in my rental house, which was vacant. My son was very upset with me and rightly so. I was taking him away from his second Mom and disrupting his life just as he was about to graduate high school. I was in significant pain but did not take pain medication for fear of developing an addiction to it. I felt alone but not isolated, even though I quit seeing our mutual friends and would often go all day not seeing or speaking to anyone.

In the midst of all this change, I asked "how can I live a spiritual life?" For about three weeks, I asked this question each time before I did anything. This included what clothes to wear, how to spend my time, and where to go. I felt wonderful, for I felt as though I was connected to Source. I was ecstatic that I was being guided through every moment. I started to see personal messages directed at me through license plates and other signs. I believed that there was a larger field of universal intelligence or consciousness and that I could access it any time I wanted. It held an answer for every question.

OBLIVIOUS

6/29/03

Moment by moment
never here
we race and do
the
time watchers
as drop
by
drop
we become more locked
bound in strait jackets
our forefathers fashioned
through each thought
action
choice
we weave our web
connected to the larger
or sticky trapped
wound encased
entombed
our choice

In April 2003, two months after the kidney surgery, a friend was leaving for California on a 6:00 am flight, so I went to the airport to talk to her before she left. I felt that I had been guided there by the Universe. Once she left, I felt that I had extraordinary powers and tried twice to get through security without a ticket. I thought that if the Universe wanted me to go somewhere it would provide the means for me to do so. However, it would not be through a miracle but rather in a normal way. As I drove back home I became convinced that the Universe was leading me again, and right before the turn to my house, I saw a truck with an attachment that makes tree limbs into mulch. I felt that I was supposed to follow this truck, which I did. I drove to Catonsville and was then directed to a small park. There I was told that radioactive canisters were leaking into the groundwater and that this pollution was moving down the watershed. I asked how far the contamination reached and was then shown how far.

I didn't hear voices. I have never heard "voices", but I have heard directives like mind tapes that one hears all the time. Voices are thoughts. I believed that these thoughts were coming to me from the Universe. I felt that this information was unquestionably true. I asked the Universe to cause me to shake each time I was traveling over radioactive contamination. I was trying to bypass my mind and any subterfuges coming from it. As I drove home, I was shaking most of the way. As I passed Fort Meade and the Naval Surface Weapons Center, I was shaking a lot. I became more and more fearful as I drove, believing that a very large area was contaminated with radioactivity. I believed that my former partner's house had radioactive soil, which deeply scared me. On the way home, there was a huge traffic jam. I believed it gave me time to see how extensive the hazardous waste pollution was. I was overcome by the size of the problem and had no idea what I was supposed to do with the knowledge.

I was fearful of the discovery of this problem and considered many options as to what to do with this information. I thought no one would believe me without tests of the water, and even then the immensity of the problem was overwhelming. I did have the local water company come and test my tap water. An incredible number of chemicals were in the water (which were deemed to be at a safe level). No tests were done, however, that would have identified toxicity from bacteria that had been affected by radioactivity and were growing in the water pipes. I believed this to be true, and later I believed that mercury chloride was in the water. I decided not to tell anyone that the water supply from Baltimore to Washington, DC, was contaminated and not safe to drink. I felt tremendous compassion for all beings in the watersheds between Baltimore and D.C., but I knew that no one would believe me. However, I started drinking bottled water from glass bottles and bought a water filtration system for my house and my son's condominium. I believed that plastic bottles leached plastic into the water and that was bad for our bodies.

My sleep at night was not good, and I meditated when I woke up, which meant several hours a night of meditation. I entered a deep state of peace during the meditations. By the end of April 2003, I had four continuous days and nights without sleep. I didn't feel tired because I was meditating during this time. I had wavering thoughts about renewing my life partnership and I decided to do so. The afternoon I decided, my estranged partner and I were together over at a mutual friend's house. I believed that our friend's house sat on ground contaminated by radioactive soil. I said nothing but firmly believed that this was true. This was a reoccurring theme: that many houses and land are contaminated with radon, which is injurious to our health. I also believed that tap water and some bottled water were contaminated. I felt that if I could send compassion into the water that would purify it. So I focused on sending compassionate thoughts into the large plastic bottle of water that was at my friend's house. I was exhausted after some time and felt that I had been exposed to large amounts of radioactivity.

That night I fell asleep at my house and woke at midnight knowing that my partner's cat died. I called her and was told that, yes, the cat had just died. I got dressed and went to her house to comfort her. On the way, there were yellow and red flashing lights. I took those as warnings not to go to her house, but I went anyway. I tried to comfort her but was not terribly successful. I was exhausted and wasn't sure I could make the drive home, so I ended staying the night upstairs. Trusty, another cat, came and licked my eyelids and treaded softly on me. In my mind, this was a sign that I was to represent the creatures of this earth in my actions and protect them. This included all creatures and also the trees. Contaminated water and earth affects all species. I decided that I should fly to Sweden and live there, because I believed that country to be more environmentally aware. I wrote a note telling my son and daughter and partner to join me there (this was taken as a suicide note at the hospital.) I couldn't sleep, so I tried sharing the bed with my former partner. I still didn't sleep and was making vibration noises, so she moved to the couch. I finally slept in the morning a few hours.

When I woke up I did not get out of bed but lay there. A part of me said that I could not move and that I was suffering from radioactive poisoning. Another part of me sat up in bed and then stood up on the floor. Then I fell back on the bed again with the part of me winning that said don't move. I didn't get up to urinate and proceeded to do so in bed on her new mattress. Part of me was aware of what I was doing and part of me couldn't move. Then I couldn't move or speak at all. I became catatonic. She dragged me out of bed on the wet sheet and left me on the floor as she proceeded to call her daughter, who is a clinical psychologist, and others. She warned me that she would take me to the hospital. My thought was that I would be the guinea pig for all those suffering from radioactivity and hazardous waste, including all species on earth. When her daughter arrived, they dressed me, and a neighbor carried me out to the car. They took me to Washington Adventist Hospital.

I had no history of mental illness and was 53 years old. When I was 24, I was depressed and saw a psychiatrist for two years but never took medication for it. One of my family members was diagnosed as a paranoid schizophrenic some twenty years ago but has never taken medication for the disorder. Another family member was diagnosed as psychotic with dementia, but I believe that for most of her life she would meet the *Diagnostic and Statistical Manual of Mental Disorders 4*[th] *Edition (DSM-IV), 1994*[2] criteria for depression and paranoid schizophrenia.[3] DSM-IV is published by the American Psychological Association and is the definitive manual for those making psychiatric diagnoses. I believe that the kidney operation brought about a chemical imbalance in my brain that caused me to live in two realities at the same time and to slip from one reality to another. After I spent approximately ten thousand dollars and saw numerous doctors, no one could verify the relationship between the kidney surgery and mental illness. First I was labeled as having depression, then bipolar with psychotic episodes, and finally schizo-affective disorder. These diagnoses are dependent on behavior. There are no blood tests or other physical tests to determine whether or not a person has a mental illness.

I did not talk as we waited in the emergency room at Washington Adventist Hospital. They gave me no food or water most of the day. They asked me to sign voluntary commitment papers. I asked what would happen if I did not. They said that if I didn't they would commit me involuntarily, and it would take longer for me to get out. I signed the paper. They took me upstairs and did paperwork on me for quite some time. It was well after midnight by the time I had a room. I was going on five days without a good night's sleep, but they didn't give me anything to help me sleep. Evidently the psychiatrist in the morning was the only one who could prescribe medication. I was put in a room with a roommate. I fell asleep only to be shaken awake about two hours later with my roommate standing over my head with a pillow and wearing shaded sunglasses. Fear leapt into my mind, and I thought I can act from fear or from love. I thanked her for bringing me a pillow and said that my pillow was enough. At that, she returned to her own bed. Meanwhile people on the ward were screaming and yelling, and there were angry voices from the staff as well as the patients. The level of fear and negativity was extremely high and loud, not conducive to sleep. I stayed awake most of that night. I kept repeating to myself that I can act from fear or love, it is my choice. I chose love.

In the morning, I saw Dr. Hardman, who prescribed medication for me. I took it and was sleepy, but I wasn't knocked out like most of the patients on the ward. I started doing yoga with my roommate and bilateral exercises. I thought that Brain Gym exercises[4] would be excellent to use with people who have mental illnesses. Unfortunately, I couldn't remember any of those exercises. There were no exercise classes, no counseling, and only one group meeting a day, which included people from both wards on the floor. This group meeting was not helpful and couldn't address individual issues because it was so large.

I talked to my roommate, and she had a son who was four when he had drowned in a swimming pool. She advised me to forgive myself for things that had happened to my son. That touched a deep cord within me. I took her advice to heart and mirrored it back to her. We had been put on the worst ward. They said there was no room on the other ward for me. The intensity of patients' screaming and yelling obscenities was scary. No staff members were there to talk to, and it seemed that no one cared about me as a person instead of a statistic. No one explained that we needed to go to a window to get medications twice a day. I interacted with my roommate and some of the other patients. Mostly though, I was confused and exhausted and felt very alone.

The second day, I noticed a line in the hallway of men waiting to come into our room, which was not permitted. I accidentally walked in on my roommate having sex in our bathroom with one of the other patients. I told the nurse, and later that night they moved me to the other, less severe ward. The next day I organized some of the patients to sing. There were about five of us singing. One patient asked if I worked there. I asked to change doctors and was able to do so. My new doctor released me the next day with a prescription of seroquel. I went back to my house. My son, although staying in the basement of the house, was rarely there.

Once I was back home, I felt that I was being guided to live in a way that substantially limited my environmental footprint. Over twenty years ago, I traveled extensively in West and East Africa. I lived in El Salvador as a Peace Corps volunteer and worked in Honduras with subsistence farming women for a year. I spent three years in Saudia Arabia teaching audio-visual techniques and equipment to the female staff of the first and only woman's college in the Eastern province. Developing country people live much closer to the margin of survival, and we are all gradually moving towards that kind of existence. Few of us in the United States of America would know how to survive without air conditioning, heat, electricity, drinkable tap water, refrigerators, cars, computers, cell phones, and the latest technology. Imagine your life without these for a week. Yet in many places of the world, these are luxury items, and the majority of people live without them. Our society's infrastructure is crumbling, and our way of life, which has been governed by greed, consumerism, and power, is not sustainable.

I believe that there is a window of opportunity to save the earth as we know it and our human species. However that window is closing. If we continue to live as we do today, the oceans will die, our food and water will be too little and too contaminated to sustain life, and our air too dirty to breathe. The earth's beauty will be destroyed and few species will continue to live. This suffering is the legacy that we are leaving to our children and grandchildren. There is so much to undo or stop that it seems overwhelming. Yet I also believe that if we can raise our soul consciousness and honor truth, honesty, compassion and love, we can help to create Eckhart Tolle's *A New Earth*.[5] The first step is to create internal peace and alignment with the Universe and then to act from that center. I did not hear voices telling me this but have watched over my lifetime the degradation of the earth and water. If humankind were to focus its energies on solving world problems (as is suggested in my book *Reinventing the University: A Radical Proposal for a Problem-Focused University*)[6], a new way of life might unfold for all species of this earth. I felt that the way I was to live my life from this time forward was as a manifestation of the Universe. To me this means flowing with unconditional love and light.

My life was to be an example to others who wanted to live in a sustainable way today. My diet contained no genetically modified organisms, and it was local and organic. My meals became smaller as uncontaminated food became sparser. I believed that our food supply was poisoned by pesticides and that we were eating our "seed corn" (limiting the variety of our food and eating that grain that would be used for seed the following year, or developing hybrids that do not provide seed for next year's crops). Our water was poisoned by lead and mercury chloride and bacteria from algae growth. It was dangerous to drink water from plastic bottles because the plastic leached into the water. The ubiquitous use of plastics that are not biodegradable fill our landfills. I tried to not use plastic but found it impossible to do so. At some point, the garbage we throw away is what we will be eating. I did not own a cell phone or television and played only selected music. I limited my intake of talk radio and did not subscribe to a newspaper. I could not figure out how not to defecate and urinate into our drinking water, so I continued to use the toilet. Through my overseas experiences, I have experienced how to live simply and in community, but it is very difficult to do so in this American competitive, entrepreneurial, consumer-oriented society. However, I also believed that the light of unconditional love is here and present and that we can make each choice from this perspective, regardless of our circumstances. I also believe that a great light is coming that will completely change our world.

The beliefs I held then were unquestionable, and I still attempt to live my life in accordance with these beliefs, although I find it difficult to change external things. My concentration turned inward to how to grow my soul and internal peace. As a meditator, I have cultivated an inner observer who steps outside of the mind and its beliefs and challenges extreme viewpoints. Even though I continued to meditate during psychotic episodes, this observer seemed to disappear. It was replaced by a tyrannical "voice" that led me to do bizarre things and masqueraded as a voice from the Universe. I tried to act from unconditional love, but sometimes fear just took over.

My son considered his basement apartment as separate from the house, and I became concerned at the friends he had developed. I had a Tibetan bell that a friend had given me, which was truly beautiful. I believed that it could energetically clear space and find negative energy and disperse it. One afternoon I took it downstairs to the basement and, by ringing the bell, was directed to a drawer where I discovered cigarettes. I trashed my son's space, including his pictures and papers. I turned over his television. Then I told him that he would have to move out of the house. I did not want to see him harm himself by smoking, particularly since he also suffered from asthma. He was very angry with me and moved out, leaving me alone.

My anchors to life were gone, as I drifted further into dual realities. The "crazy" thoughts always carried a kernel of truth but would spin out into a whole thought pattern that I did not question, because I thought I was being directed by the Universe. The thoughts would come like waves. I insisted on carrying purified water in glass bottles because I knew that tap water was contaminated and plastic bottles leached plastic into the water. There were few outward signs that my beliefs were all-encompassing and strange. I could function fairly well in everyday reality, although I was still weak from the surgery and withdrawn. Beliefs came to me like waves that would come and then recede, but always staying in the background. My daughter was graduating from Indiana University in Pennsylvania at the end of May, but I knew I couldn't make the trip to attend her graduation. Physically I was still very weak, and I was afraid of spoiling her graduation with my bizarre behavior. My former partner and her daughter tried to get me to go, but I smashed a coffee cup in anger when they would not listen to me. I rarely showed any displays of anger, but this time I did. They finally left to go to the graduation ceremony without me. I felt very sad that I could not attend the graduation ceremony.

I stopped my medication in July but continued having weekly acupuncture sessions and weekly energetic counseling sessions. I saw many doctors to try to determine what had caused the psychotic event. This search included doctors versed in alternative and allopathic medicine: an endocrinologist, an environmental specialist, a dentist, and a cadre of others who helped me to detoxify my body of heavy metals. But no one had the answer as to why I had a psychotic episode.

My beliefs about relationships and the Universe as outlined at the end of April 2003 were as follows.

1. Ask for guidance in every action I take, with the intention that it will be for the highest good of all beings. Listen, hear, act, and let go of the outcome.
2. Trust my intuition and the Universe. There are other ways of knowing. Never question feelings, always question the beliefs that underlie them.
3. Strive to be congruent and in alignment. Gut, heart, mind in alignment with spirit and soul purpose in everything. Feelings point towards beliefs. With each feeling comes a belief or series of beliefs. The only way to get rid of the pain is by opening to it, feeling it, extracting the information about the belief that supports it, questioning the belief with your higher wisdom and letting go.

4. Security and safety is received by letting go of everything and trusting in the Universe.
5. Life is beautiful and I am filled with thankfulness and gratitude at the gift of just being here.
6. We are meant to live the fullness of our being, which means the greatest sorrow and the greatest joy, but we will not stay in either.
7. Habits, patterns, and routines preclude possibilities and limit choice.
8. I can be whole no matter what I've experienced if I accept that there is purpose, trust in the Universe, and let go of trying to control life.
9. One must come to peace within oneself before there can be peace in the world.
10. I am responsible for the choices I make. Whichever choice I make is the perfect choice for my own soul's growth.

I wrote a sermon to be presented at my Unitarian Universalist Church on May 4, 2003. However, instead of presenting it in church, I ended up living it behind the locked doors of a psychiatric ward. The text is given below.

> To an outside observer my life over the past year could be described as being in a strong undertow. However, for me this has been the richest, hardest, most painful, most uplifting, most challenging and most awesome year of my life. Old identities, patterns and beliefs have been dissolving as I have been brought into a realignment at all levels. As Eckhart Tolle said in his book, *The Power of Now,* "death is a stripping away of all that is not you. The secret of life is to die before you die and find that there is no death."[7] I believe that this is true. This past year has been one of tremendous spiritual seeking for me. I feel as though I have been pared down to my essence, an essence or energy that is intimately connected to everyone and everything. There's nothing like staring death in the face to give you clarity about who you are, what is important in life and deep gratitude for life itself. Maybe that is death's greatest value.

I believe that the only life we ever really have is this present moment and that we can choose how we act, think, and are in this moment. We can't choose what happens to us, but we can choose our attitude towards it, how we think about it, and what we do. I believe we make our choices from fear or love. There generally is no one right choice; life is much too complex for that. At any given moment we have lots of choices and each choice carries consequences, not only for us but also for every other being. I am learning to watch the consequences of my actions, and if I don't like the consequences that are apparent to me then I can make a different choice when a similar situation occurs. I don't need to act from habit or reaction. Do we make our choices with the intent that they are for the highest good of all beings? It's the choices that we make in daily life that define who we are and it's our beliefs that drive our choices. Do I choose to interact with a smile and from love, or unconsciously dismiss the person because I'm too busy, or too insecure?

I have learned that my feelings and emotions point to beliefs, often underlying childhood beliefs that are not true but have ruled my life because they were unconscious. Before I discovered the tumor, I was caught in a whirlpool of fear around whether I could be a successful small business owner and financially make it. Many of my choices derived from my feelings of unworthiness and the unconscious belief that life was not my birthright. With the tumor, I was suddenly catapulted from my anxieties and fear about money and jobs to confronting death and from there to a realization that I am worthy as I am. I now have a tremendous gratitude for my life.

In recovering from the surgery, I have been forced to stop my frenetic pace, just stop. That has given me very different perspectives on life. Some may say that I have been in a huge undertow. All I can say is that I am very thankful each morning to be alive, and I choose to be fully present to whatever is happening and to what I am feeling. Most of my life I have resisted the whirlpool of feelings, repressed them and struggled to swim straight in against the riptide. I didn't know there was another way. But there is! Our feelings need to be felt and acknowledged for they point to our underlying and often unconscious beliefs which need to be questioned. By going through what I have experienced and approaching it as a learning I have been given insights that I would never have gained otherwise. I have found my heart's passion in practicing acupressure.[8]

I now feel as though I am carried by the Universe and am developing a deep trust that it will and does take care of me on a very practical level, if I will listen, act, trust and let go of the outcome. I ask that my choices be directed by the Universe which I regard as the underlying implicate order or an all-encompassing force field of compassion. I believe that this surrendering of choice allows me to co-create my reality with a much greater consciousness. I feel in the flow with joy and gratitude in my heart. I still experience all emotions—fear, anger, sadness, anxiety, grief. However, on a good day I feel them, acknowledge them, understand what assumptions underlie them and move through them. What's enabled me to do this? Grace and a willingness to drop my illusion that I can control anything except the choices I make and that I can choose grace.

What have I learned from May 2002-May 2003, including the pain I have experienced? I have learned to be in the present with thankfulness. I have learned to go into feelings to go through them. I have learned to not ignore the pain but go into it and accept it and be with it. I have learned that I have a choice to live in fear and doubt or trust and love. I watch my reactions and motivations and attempt to understand why I choose what I do. I now accept the paradox that what I choose matters and that the consequence of the choices I make are exactly what I need to provide me with opportunities to deepen my soul learnings—which for me are what life is all about anyway. I also understand that my consciousness is not as big as that of the Universe. My mind will never be able to accurately grasp why things happen as they do. I do believe though that the Universe presents me with what is good for the growth of my soul, not what I think is best or right! I am now seeking to live this new life by expanding my awareness, accessing my inner power through connection, and making conscious choices. I trust that the Universe holds and supports me, and I hold myself and others with lots of compassion as we move together through this ocean of life.

This sermon explains my mindset at the beginning of May 2003. In the month before, I became increasingly sensitive to all sensory input. It seemed that my intuition was very present and led me to synchronistic events. I intuitively changed my diet and went to a nutritionist for her advice. She responded that all I was taking was exactly what she would have suggested for me. I was aware of the energetic vibration of song, movie images, television, and cell phones, and was too sensitive to listen to or to watch them. I felt frequency vibrations at night and covered my windows with metal shielding tarps so I could sleep at night. Lights from police cars, ambulances, fire engines, tow trucks, and school buses would, and still do, make me cringe. I'm not as sensitive now, which may be the result of medication I am taking. I looked upon myself then as a canary in a mine. I was aware of things that are injurious to people, they just don't know it.

I know that my mind, body, emotions and spirit are all interconnected. Whatever affects one affects all. As soon as I could after surgery, I joined a class in the County swimming pool for people with arthritis. I was unable to swim at this time because my body was very weak and not healed from the surgery. After a year in the arthritis class, I could swim laps in the pool and signed up for a water aerobics class that met three times per week. There was time to socialize during class and talk to people. At this time I had no other connection to people. Four years later, I am still taking the water aerobics class and swimming 30 lengths. I also joined a group that did sacred circle dancing. The steps were difficult for me. My brain had difficulty making the correct movements but the group was patient and supported me. I felt as though the neurons were remaking their neural pathways. I stopped the dancing after a year because it was too difficult for me.

A friend of mine practices shamanic healing.[9] This type of healing was pervasive throughout the world thousands of years ago and is still practiced with some indigenous populations and other shamanic healers. Since 2004 she has led shamanic journey groups and individual sessions that have helped me to connect with my own spirituality and release negative energy in a constructive way. From a shamanic point of view, soul loss (loss of self), power loss (loss of connection to Universe), and energy blocks are the major causes of illness brought about by separation or trauma. She has used rituals and ceremonies that have helped me to feel my inner power. She has led me through shamanic rituals and journeying. Shamanism is a method of knowing, of having a direct experience with mystery. It is not a religion or faith. I believe the deepest healings have occurred because of her depth of compassion and her deep connection with the Loving and Compassionate Spirits of the Universe.

For a shaman, a part of the soul leaves when you experience a trauma, including surgery. A shamanic practitioner can journey to retrieve the lost soul part and return it to you. This journey usually involves rattles, drums, dancing, and singing on the part of the practitioner, while the client lies down silently. I have experienced other shamanic rituals of empowerment, forgiveness, and letting go of negativity. Teresa has established a shamanic journey group in which a group of people come together twice a month and dance and sing in a circle around a candle. Each person sets their intention and then lies down while Teresa maintains a drumbeat. The classic shamanic journey is a simple technique that has been practiced on all continents for at least 40,000 years. The shamanic journey is an individual's contact with Mystery or the Universe and brings forth that connection.

I also supported my return to a healthy body through taking yoga. I started with gentle yoga and proceeded with Anusara yoga[10]. This yoga is about opening the body to grace, and I continue to feel a joy that comes with this type of Hatha yoga. [11]

Right after the kidney surgery, I started getting acupuncture,[12] jin shin jiytsu,[13] clinical and Process Acupressure,[14] and bodywork therapy. These forms of bodywork deal with all aspects of a person. For the last six years, I have received these forms of bodywork, which also treat the mind, emotions and soul. In October 2007, I received two certifications and state licenses for 795 hours of shiatsu and massage therapy.[15] I believe that all of these activities have helped me maintain a level of health. My body responds very well to touch, and I believe I was able to stay out of the hospital as much as I did because I made a concerted effort to fully take care of my body.

By July 2003, I stopped taking my medication because I believed that it was harming my body, and I did not think I had a mental illness. The side effects were relatively minor, but I didn't want to tax my body further. I did not see much of a difference when I stopped the seroquel. I was on the lowest dosage of seroquel. I still lived in a dual reality but did not share any of my thoughts with others. Sometimes I understood what actions might be perceived as "crazy" and did not engage in those when people were around me. I believed I was being guided by the Universe. There appeared to be a vast intelligence that was not the Universe, Tao, or God. This broad spectrum knew everything. It seemed that I had access to this intelligence and could ask it anything. I did not question my thoughts or their origins as they solidified into beliefs that I acted on. I was trying to take good care of myself. I was on a regimen of supplements that one doctor had prescribed, along with colonics and heavy metal detoxicants.

MY DESTINY

8/31/03

It came
like the tornado whirling ever larger
and threw me against the wall
this side
and
that
Teeth shaken loose
hair on end
body afire
blinded
and confused
caught on a
high speed train
traveling far
from everything
I once knew
from all my self-images
relationships
identities
anchors
Then pushed off
falling
into the unknown
I lay broken
on the railway bed
in an unknown land
monsters loomed
from all my fears
and blackness
of my own creation
but held
in deeper love and light

living choice
with awareness
knowing I create my reality
fear or love
perceptions dissolving
reforming
feelings buried
now unleashed
until
I learn how
to gently hold them
Surrender
to co-create
the laying down of ego
and identity
to be
oneness
and hold
with strength
my new self
and grow it
water it
nurture it
love it
be it
This is my path now
Response to signs
Learning this new life
Sensing others' energy
but not entangling
disentangling
cutting free
to be fully
me

In the summer of 2003, I moved in and out of my day-to-day reality and a much vaster reality. On one occasion, I danced in the shower while thinking that I was in a dancing competition with an Indian spiritual teacher. I then thought that the male gods of Olympus were oppressing women, but that I had the upper hand. I cut off part of the waistband on a pair of trousers for no apparent reason and then walked naked outside, down my sidewalk and back. I wrote notes and posted them on water containers that the water was toxic. Some had microscopic algae that produced toxins and some had mercury chloride. I had a white albino catfish in an aquarium. He was my pet of four years and my only companion most of the time. As my belief grew that the water he swam in was increasingly toxic, I almost intentionally killed my fish so he wouldn't have a slow death. Thankfully I realized that there was an alternative, and I took him to Lilypons, a place that has decorative ponds. They were happy to take him. It scared me though that I had almost killed him. I realized how beliefs could lead to harming others.

I researched on the internet the number of toxic chemicals that science has produced and what is in our water supply system. I even talked to a scientist about pfisteria and how he believed that it was caused by a lack of oxygen in the water. Not only have we poisoned the water we drink, but we have also poisoned it for all species. Whoever decided that we should urinate and defecate into the water we drink, or use water as a dumping ground for pesticides, prescription drugs, and toxic chemicals?

I was so sensitive to vibrations, sensory stimuli, and radio frequencies that I rarely left my house the summer of 2003. I bought tarps to hang in my bedroom to keep out the frequencies so I could sleep at night. I could feel vibrations from computers and printers and from fluorescent lights. I spent most of my time seeing doctors, which did not help me. It was very difficult for me to pay bills and keep track of my finances. I spent money without thinking. I felt that my house had a lot of negative energy in it and wanted to move. I looked at property on

Slaughter Beach in Delaware thinking to build a house. I eliminated that option when I saw the pollution and dead fish and wildlife on the beach.

I signed up for a conference/workshop that was held in September by a spiritual leader. I had discovered that he was looking for a new staff member, and I sent an application for the position. I didn't hear back from them, so I called and was told that I was being considered for the job. However, I heard nothing official from them. I decided to go to the workshop and then on to their headquarters in Oregon. I had shared with them that I had a psychotic episode. I went to the workshop and functioned quite well. Then I flew to Oregon and had an all-day drive. I broke the trip by staying at a motel. The next morning I was seeing personal signs to me such as the star at the Texaco station, which I interpreted as a sign of good fortune. I had trouble sleeping again but arrived that afternoon. I had arranged to stay at a bed and breakfast recommended to me by a friend.

I liked the town and spent two days with a real estate agent looking at houses to buy. I managed to get an interview, but it didn't go well, and I broke down crying twice during it. I went to a spa where I was going to have a hot stone treatment and became afraid. I saw the reflections of bars on the wall inside the steam room and translated that to mean that if I stayed I would be locked up. So I cancelled the massage and packed and left town. I felt panic, and the town seemed to become menacing instead of welcoming. On my way out of town, I stopped by a stream that has lithium salts in it and drank from the stream.

I then drove to Crater Lake, which was beautiful. I stood by the edge and thought that if I yelled, this promontory would break off and open a hole in the side of the crater that would cause devastation. I stayed by the edge for several hours as catastrophic visions surfaced in my mind. I finally left as it was dark. I drove several hours to the motel that I had stopped at on my way down. I was exhausted and hungry. I ate a piece of blueberry pie from the café next door and went to bed.

The next day I woke up early and skipped breakfast. As I drove back to Portland, I stopped twice. I stopped at a small road off the major highway. I was sure that Crater Lake was going to erupt and that there would be intense ash and a fireball. I took off my contacts and set them inside a mail box, not even in a container. Then I drove the car, almost completely blind, about fifty feet up the road and parked it. I then went into the woods and found a tree to sit under. I was sure that the volcano would erupt soon so I started wrapping vines around me to connect me to the tree. The thought was when the tree was uprooted I would go with it. Then I started saying a metta or loving-kindness prayer. It was a Buddhist prayer of loving-kindness that I had embellished:

More and more may I be filled with loving kindness and mindfulness

More and more may I have compassion for myself and others

More and more may I be filled with the love, joy, peace, and energy of the Universe

More and more may I be physically, mentally, spiritually, and emotionally whole and balanced

More and more may I be aware of my feelings and process them

More and more may I live in the present moment, making decisions for the seventh generation

More and more I am thankful for everything I experience

I felt that if I could say this prayer out loud it could save humankind. But I couldn't miss a word. I believed that I was the last person on earth to say this and save the earth. All the other people, dead and alive, who had tried to say this prayer had failed. I also believed that those who had almost said it correctly died and came back into this world with a disability so they could truly learn what compassion means. An airplane flew over several times, and I thought the plane had a bomb with nuclear warhead that would be dropped into Crater Lake. After three or four hours in the woods, I felt that my thoughts about the catastrophe were wrong. The fact that the catastrophe did not occur changed my thoughts to "it will still happen, but at a later time." I made my way back to the road, and thankfully my contacts were still in the mail box. I met a man who lived nearby, and we had a short conversation about my walk in the woods and where we both were from. I only realized later that my hair was scraggly with pieces of leaves and vines. I also discovered later that I had left my beautiful Tibetan bell under the tree. It was very precious to me, and it added to a pervasive sense of loss. I was afraid, exhausted, and hungry.

I drove back toward the highway and stopped to eat dinner. As I was eating, a fly walked across my plate. I believed that this fly was warning me not to eat what it walked upon. This food would not be good for me. I also saw a post card of a lighthouse with no light and believed that my son, who collects pictures of lighthouses, was dead. I felt the full emotional impact of that and had to leave the restaurant without eating. I took a piece of pie with me. I saw a homeless man sitting on the stoop in front of MacDonald's. I asked if he wanted my pie, which he took. I also gave him some money for dinner. I felt so strongly that I could be him—homeless and alone. We sat together for a few minutes as he told me his story about hitch-hiking to get to his father who was very ill. My heart opened as I realized "there but for the grace of God go I."

I continued on my journey and was realizing that if I did not drive through the night I would miss my flight home. So I drove on. I stopped at a rest stop to get a little sleep. Large trucks were parked next to me, and I kept thinking that they would run over my car. As I sat in the car trying to sleep and feeling the fear, I imagined that I had crossed the barrier between sleeping and waking states. My dreams became my waking reality, and my ordinary reality became my dreams. After a few hours, I decided to drive on knowing that I had already probably missed my plane.

In Portland, I stopped at a gas station, and the thought came to me that I could go back in time and be 20 again with my life in front of me or stay 53 with the wisdom I had gained in life. I chose to stay my same age. When I arrived at the airport, it looked strange to me. Everyone I saw seemed to have a disability of some sort. I believed that the earth there was toxic, full of uranium and toxic waste. I proceeded to the check in for my airline and took out my contacts and threw them away. I did not have any glasses or spare pair of contacts. I had no idea why I was to throw away my contacts, but I was directed to do so. A flight was leaving for Baltimore-Washington International Airport (BWI) right then, so I was able to make it. We landed in Chicago, and I couldn't read the arrival/departure displays so I asked someone for help. A stranger kindly helped me find my plane.

When I arrived in BWI, it was one of the last planes in for the night. By this time, I was completely exhausted and hungry. I left my laptop computer at the airport along with my carry-on luggage. I got on one of the buses and huddled in the back seat, trying to sleep. The bus just circled between the airport and satellite parking. The bus driver came back and woke me up and said that I needed to get off. He found a taxi for me. I gave the taxi my former business address. Once we were close, I asked him to stop, and I got out and hugged a tree. The taxi stayed there. Realizing that I didn't have a key to my office, I got back in and gave him my home address. He told me it would cost $150 for the trip, so I had him stop by an automatic teller machine so I could pay him. I felt wary around him, not sure that he would take me home. He did though, and I got out and went to my neighbor's house, which had a light on. Once he had driven away, I went to my house. My son, who was to pick me up at the airport, was worried sick. I didn't have a cell phone and wasn't capable of calling him at the airport. When we talked, he went to pick up my laptop and bag, which the police were holding.

A day or two later, I was walking close to the house and started talking out loud about environmental issues and how we are all destroying our environment. No one was present to listen to my diatribe, but I believed that what I was saying was being broadcast to people, like telepathy. I believed that the words were coming through me from a larger Source. I then lay down in the grass and imagined that I was being spied upon by someone, military or extraterrestrial, from planes overhead. As long as I lay perfectly still, they couldn't see me, but if I moved they could identify me. I stayed lying in the grass for a long time. Finally I got up and went to hug a tree. I hugged several of them and then realized that I was being approached by two policemen and a policewoman. They asked me questions and I repeated what they were asking me. This disconcerted them. At one point I mentioned extraterrestrials, and at that they put me in a cruiser and took me to Montgomery General

Hospital. They placed me under observation. I shut down and quit interacting with anyone. Due to my history, my insurance, and lack of available space, I was transported to Washington Adventist Hospital. It was October 1, 2003, and they kept me until October 6th.

Once more, they placed me in the ward with the most severe cases. There was screaming and yelling, and the staff appeared angry and fearful except for one man. I now knew the drill of coming to get my medication, but I did not take it, even though they looked inside my mouth. This time they gave me all kinds of medication. I did not want to be a zombie as most of the other patients were. Because the blood tests they took daily showed no sign of the medications, they gave me shots of medications. I did not know if it was day or night for several days. The only memories I have were looking out the window at sunset (or sunrise), I didn't know which. I was drugged, so I could not do anything but sleep. I felt as though I had no control over anything. I was being forced against my will to take medications that I believed were harmful to me. I was afraid and scared of the staff. I thought again how my fearful dream world had become my living reality. Some days we were allowed outside on the roof for awhile to shoot baskets, or walk around, or even dance. I loved those times. I hated being inside with no contact with the elements and trees.

When I was a little better, I suggested to the other patients that we could swap food so none of it would be wasted. Most of us started doing that. A television was always on during mealtime, blaring in the background. One guy on the ward liked to sing, so we would sing together as we walked up and down the hallway. I paced out how many steps there were to the locked door so that I could walk it blindly. I kept thinking of how to escape. At one point, I thought if I put my clothes on top of the trash cart it would be carried out through the locked door, and somehow I would get away too. Needless to say I lost my clothes and remained a prisoner. In talking to other patients, I found out that two of them had been to Oak Ridge, Tennessee. We all were aware that this location produced and stored radioactive hazardous waste. I thought that this was the reason we all had been hospitalized. We knew too much.

I had Dr. Hardman again and asked to change physicians. I felt that he had no compassion and was never available to talk or interact with me. I had no trust in him. After several days they let me change doctors. There was still no one except other patients to talk to. The staff took vital signs and blood at least once a day. It hurt when they took blood. I struggled with the fear of being there and pain from the kidney operation. These were dark days, and yet I tried to connect with the patients. A younger woman, Susan, was taken to a padded room next to the nurse's station. She put her arm right through the glass door to the nurse's station and cut herself badly. She was then taken out to another part of the hospital. A young woman, Mary, was voluntarily committed and was very afraid of being on the ward. Mary thought that the staff was trying to kill her. I got the telephone number of someone in the hospital who was an advocate for the mentally ill and told her of the situation with Mary. She left the next day.

FALLING LEAVES

10/27/03

Rain,
cold drippy
leaves sog and fall with their weight
waiting beyond the naked trees
glowing eyes in the dark
held by charcoal embers
that will not die
Who and what am I
What is my essence
that lasts
when the last leaf
falls
the last leaves
and I stay
broken, humbled, labeled
victim
I don't want to be
How not to?
live within the fear without becoming a part of it
I need a lot of practice and
heartfelt support
drip
drip
away

Shortly after I got out of the hospital, my daughter came to live with me. Her fiancé was in Iraq, and she became a stabilizing force for me. I was taking seroquel in a higher dosage and continued to search for the cause of changes in my behavior. I did not think of myself as having a mental illness but rather changes in brain chemistry that would cause me to think and act in socially unacceptable ways.

One night I left my house and went for a walk in the neighborhood. I believed that the earth was suffering and that many species were already extinct and many more would be shortly, including the human species. I saw five lights, which I believed to be signs that there were five of us who could save the planet. One by one, the lights went out until there were only two lights left. I felt that one of the lights represented me and the other an enlightened being from India. I then thought that I was being given a choice: I could stay on earth and spend the rest of my life in an insane asylum or I could go to Mars or some far away planet and continue the human species by coupling with the enlightened being there. I said "yes" to Mars and then walked back toward my house.

As I approached a little woods at the side of my house I saw back porch lights. I believed these lights were Martians or other extraterrestrials. I spent a long time looking at them as the lights dissolved into microscopic life forms. I was a cat watching them and wondering how and when they would scoop me up and take me with them. I took off my shoes and socks and slithered on my belly through the trees and brush to get a closer look. At one point I looked at my house where many lights were on and I could see people moving about. My daughter was now staying with me, but there were other people in the house as well. I was outside for hours thinking that I was going to leave everything that I knew and loved. That seemed to be the only way to save humankind and other species.

I cared deeply then, as I do now, about the environment, Mother Earth, and all beings. I felt the sense of interdependence with all, a web of life. Since 1993 I had, for the most part, followed the Buddhist tenet of not killing creatures. I did find this difficult where insects were concerned. However, this deep flood of connection now filled me, and my heart ached at the suffering caused to so many creatures. I worried about water being contaminated for all beings. I felt that trees were and are living beings. I intuited that the human species is the lowest form of intelligence on earth because we do not know how to live in harmony with our environment and other species. Trees are of the highest form and then dolphins, whales, and birds.

We humans have not learned to live in peace and harmony, as most other species do. I felt that somehow I would be able to change this in order to save the human species. I realized that we Americans have constructed our lives in such a way that environmental degradation is all around us. Our lifestyles with cars and trucks, developers and miners who strip the land, the ubiquitous use of plastics, and the creation of toxic chemicals and nuclear warfare join together to destroy the beautiful earth we know. I thought that as species here on earth become extinct, they are transformed and transported to another planet.

For the human species to be transported to another planet requires that we learn how to be present in the moment and at peace within ourselves and with everything around us. After several hours in the small woods, I was cold and mentally exhausted. I was ready to give up everything, and now it seemed the Martians were not going to take me away. I found the crook of the tree where I had left my shoes and socks and put on my shoes, leaving my wet socks in the crook of the tree, and went home. By now it was just my daughter there. I didn't say anything to her as I went to my bedroom to get some sleep.

On July 1, 2004, I quit taking seroquel. I was seeing a doctor who was prescribing amino acids and supplements. Many times I seemed to be swallowed up by fear. I was trying to learn how, with my counselor, to stay and face the fear. I continued with what I perceived was a fairly normal life. In March I assumed a part time position in research administration through a friend of mine at a nearby university. I had worked in this profession for sixteen years, and prior to this position, I was an Associate Director in charge of a staff of thirty-two people. I was very well aware of my limitations then in 2004 and now. My thoughts were still that I was being directed by the Universe. I was reticent with other people in the office, and my dress was not professional enough. I was in a cubicle next to two other people whom I enjoyed. At the end of August, they gave me a private office. I kept the fluorescent lights off and placed diodes on the computer and printer to eliminate harmful vibrations. I became more reclusive.

From my journal on August 20, 2004, I wrote the following.

> What if it is all about living in the moment, (Eckhart Tolle's *Power of Now*)[16]. Keeping the mind detached, and out of the present and past. Bringing consciousness into everything—choices, feelings, actions. If I am the Universe in a holographic way then my learning, my ability to hold this consciousness would benefit all. Maybe it is not about what I do but how I do it. How am I living my life in each moment? Can I not worry about the future, can I let go of the past, can I stop defending and let go of my false identities and understand that who I am is my essence—a grounded light being? Then taking care of myself becomes the most important thing I can do and how I do that in relationship with other beings in my world. Are souls transitioning in quickly (to help increase the consciousness) to break the old energetic patterns—belief systems, but more importantly identification with the mind? Is it a race, with the end result the survival, or not, of the human species? So much to know and it doesn't matter if I ever know. That is not my task. I just need to be here, now.

My daughter got married on August 28, 2004. I did little of the preparation, but was there for the wedding in Pennsylvania. It was a wonderful event, and I did feel shaky and stressed as well as happy for the couple. Two weeks later, I called my younger brother from work, and we talked about the fact that both of us were under surveillance. We assumed the phone was tapped and that someone was listening to our conversation. It was freeing to have him agree with me. We talked for a good hour. Then I wrote an e-mail to two graduate students submitting a letter of resignation. I also sent a copy to my old boss and the President of the non-profit I had previously worked for. Then I left the office.

By this time, my thoughts were that I was being followed and that a hurricane was on its way. I went home and gathered up a lovely teapot I had bought with 2 cups, my best earrings, and a scarf and took them to friends' houses. They weren't home, so I left the gifts inside their screen doors. I stopped and called my son, telling him I was on the way to the airport. He asked me to come to his workplace first. As I was driving there, I was consumed by panic that I was being watched and that there was a police car stopping traffic, waiting to find me. I was directed by my thoughts, my intuition, to travel back roads to get to his workplace. Then I ended up at a little park next to a school. I was sure by this time that I was being followed and tracked by planes. I got out of the car and stuffed my purse into a nearby trash can. Then I tried to hide in a hole made by a dead tree. I realized I wouldn't fit, so I went into some underbrush and lay on the ground. My heart was beating wildly and I was sure that the military or extraterrestrials were going to kill me. They could track me by any metal that I was wearing. So I took off my wedding ring that my former partner had given to me and threw it away. I pulled more brush on top of me and small tree limbs so I couldn't be seen. I lay there for hours. I believed that whoever was tracking me could send laser beams down that could kill me. However, if I shook and vibrated, that would save me. I lay there shaking and completely taken over by fear. I finally urinated in my clothes and thought that that indicated that I was really dead.

Then it seemed that I was alive and had eluded them. It was now night time. I crawled out from the brush and took off my filthy clothes. The night was warm. I tried to make my way back to my car but couldn't find it. The thoughts in my head said, "look and act crazy. If you do that, no one will hurt you." I walked out and onto a street that ended in a cul-de-sac. I saw the lights inside cars indicating that the alarm system was on but I took it to mean that someone was in the car watching me. In order not to be taken away by them, I started yelling to the houses on the street about the environment. I gave a diatribe on how we were destroying our environment and how much energy was being used to light houses.

Not long after two police cars appeared. I had come out of my state somewhat and asked the police for a jacket or blanket or anything that

I could use to cover up. They ignored my request and continued to ask me questions. Sitting naked on the curb, I shut down and didn't talk. It was about twenty minutes before the ambulance arrived, and they bundled me up in a blanket and took me away to Holy Cross Hospital. I was afraid and confused. At one point I got angry, and they put me in restraints—hard, leather cuffs that dug into my feet and hands. I thought that I had died and come back to life, only to suffer more in the "killing factories," as I called the hospitals. They transferred me to Washington Adventist September 8, 2004, where my doctor once again was Dr. Hardman. This time the diagnosis was bipolar disorder with psychosis.[17]

I was locked behind a set of two double doors, sharing a room with a woman who thought that al Qaida insurgents were everywhere. I got along with her fine. I had a deep sense of fear that the atmosphere provoked. I went to the medication window twice a day to receive medication but did not take it. My bizarre behavior persisted. They started giving me intramuscular shots. I paced the halls and talked to some of the patients. I went to a church service and sang hymns. I longed for the days when we could go outside. Even though it was for a short time it was a chance for fresh air and movement. I shot baskets and could look out and see the tree tops below.

Our large group meetings were not useful to me, and there were no other planned activities or counseling. They moved me into the observation room with a camera. I bundled up in blankets and tried to sleep on the floor so the camera couldn't see me. At one point I remember hallucinating with my eyes closed watching pilgrims march around the Ka'bah in Mecca. Perhaps I saw this because one of the patients was a devout Muslim speaking his prayers five times a day, or maybe it was because I had spent three years in Saudi Arabia at King Faisal University as Head of the Audio-Visual Department. It seemed that I was light years away from my previous life.

One night, five men came in to give me my medication. It seemed like overkill. I was angry at this and kicked the medicine tray, sending the meds flying. In retaliation, they held me down and gave me a shot of atavan, a muscle relaxant. They gave me an overdose, and immediately all of my muscles relaxed, and I fell back onto the bed not able to move a muscle. They gave me shots of atavan several times, and there were no further displays of anger on my part. My foot bled and was bruised, but no one looked at it. I believed that the medications they wanted me to take were poisons that would hurt my body. I had requested changing doctors and after a number of days was able to do so. When I was discharged after 12 days, my stepmother had flown up from Texas to take care of me.

She looked after me and supervised me taking my medication. But just as I had not taken the medications in the hospital, I did not take them at home. I finally admitted this to her, and she became very angry with me. Meanwhile, I was living in two realities again. My behavior was not bizarre, but I secretly planned my escape from the extraterrestials who were watching me and flying over my house in airplanes. I packed two shoulder yoga bags with necessities and a few clothes. When my stepmother left to get her hair done, I called a cab. I went to the bank and withdrew $10,000 in cash and threw out my original birth certificate and other identification so I couldn't be tracked. The cab then took me to my former place of business, where I talked to my former business partner. I told her I was going somewhere but said I didn't know where, which was the truth. I then hailed a cab and went to the metro station.

From there I took the train to Union Station in Washington, DC, and bought a covered blindfold before catching a train to Penn Station in New York. I believed that supernatural entities could track me by seeing what I was seeing and hearing what I heard. Thus I donned the blindfold and ear plugs and sang under my breath each time a stop was announced. When I reached Penn Station, I bought a ticket to Montreal and paid for it by credit card. It was late and the train didn't leave until morning, so I tried to find a hotel. It was difficult because most of them were full. I finally found one and walked the several blocks to it. I checked in, paying with cash, so they charged me an extra $100. The room had mirrors everywhere. I didn't turn on the lights or look at the mirrors. I felt that it was not safe to look in any mirrors. I slept some of the night then awakened and went to the subway not asking for my $100 back from the hotel clerk.

On the way, I stopped at a store and bought a red skirt from India that had mirrors sewn into it and a black leather jacket. I then rode around on the subway all day. I came up twice from the underground. The first time, two very kind women who were proselytizing their fundamentalist religion gave me some water and helped direct me into a restaurant where I could use the rest room. The second time, I stopped for some food. In the late afternoon, I went back to Penn Station. I caught a train to Poughkeepsie, not Montreal. It was cool and rainy there, but I had left my new jacket on a subway car. I checked into a hotel after arranging with a taxi driver to pick me up at 4:00 a.m. I ate dinner and slept until about 3:00 a.m. I then got up and went to look for the taxi. He didn't come, but another one did. I asked if he would take me to JFK airport.

He drove me to JFK, and we went to Aero Mexico. I walked up to the counter and bought a ticket for the next flight, which happened to be to Mexico City. I tried to keep from looking at anything that would give away where I was. I believed that the extraterrestrials could see out of my eyes, and if there were identifying signs, they could come and harm me. Therefore it was very important to be aware of what I was looking at. I flew to Mexico City and stayed in the airport all day without going through customs.

In the early evening, I checked in at Air France and bought a ticket to Paris. I then ate dinner. I slept some on the plane. When I arrived in Paris, I took a shuttle bus to another terminal and then got off. I walked up to the nearest ticket counter and said that I wanted a ticket. I didn't know where I was going. They took my passport and took me to a back room, where they gave me a visa for Madagascar. The flight left shortly, and I spent the next eleven hours on the plane. I softly cried on the plane, not knowing why. I slept some.

When I arrived in the capital of Madagascar, I was afraid that customs wouldn't let me through, but there was no problem. I was only carrying a small yoga bag and purse. The custom guards even remarked that I was traveling very light. I took a cab to a hotel whose name I got from the man in front of me in line. I checked in and paid for the night. I slept a few hours and thought that the sirens outside were people looking for me. I got up and took a cab to another hotel. I checked in, but the room wasn't ready so I walked around the neighborhood. I ran into a young man who said that I should go to island Saint Marie. He sold me a map and gave me a description of the island. Again I thought I was being guided by the Universe, so I headed for the van that could take me across the country to the coast. The vans were similar to ones that I had traveled in when I was in El Salvador and Africa. You sit and wait until the van is full and then you go. The van was parked on the edge of a shanty town, and children were playing in the sewage. My heart swelled with compassion that poor people were living in such bad conditions. In the late afternoon, the van left.

I enjoyed looking out the window watching the countryside go by. Once out of the city, the van stopped every few kilometers as it crossed a bridge made of wooden planks. As it became dark, I thought that we stopped for the police to check our papers. By moving my head side to side behind the front chair, I was stopping any surveillance technology that the police had. I proceeded to do this almost the whole trip.

I believe that everyone else in the van was noting my strange behavior, but I didn't have this realization then. We stopped to eat dinner and someone ordered me some soup, which I ate with relish. I don't know how long it took to reach the coast, but once there, a French couple saw to it that I had a room of my own in a hotel. Again I didn't look at any mirrors and tried to keep my eyes closed as I moved about the room and took a shower. I awoke about 5:00 a.m. and left the hotel by a side door.

I walked to the beach a few blocks away and waited for the bus that was sitting there empty to go somewhere. The driver was cleaning it and told me it would be a little while. He said he could then take me to where another bus would take me further north to catch a boat to Saint Marie Island. I waited, looking out over the harbor. I could see some ships, and the ocean water didn't look very clean. I sat on the beach watching the ocean. After a while, the bus driver said he was ready. I told him that I needed to go to a bank to exchange some money. He took me to a bank, but it wasn't open yet. I saw two men who offered to exchange my money, and so I exchanged all the money that I had. They held back some money, and I pretended to count it. (I knew that I could not actually count it because my thinking was so fuzzy.) Then they gave me some more money. I resumed my trek with the bus driver, and he dropped me off at a bus stop with vans again. When the van was full, off we went.

I sat in the front seat between the driver and a woman. The woman seemed to act as though she was above everybody else and my intuition (Universe?) told me to not trust her. Several hours later, I needed to urinate, and she wasn't going to let me out of the van. I climbed into the back seat and out as other passengers did the same. I resumed my seat afterwards.

She saw that my purse was overflowing with money, and I felt that she was dangerous to me. I had the thought to throw away my glasses so everyone would think I was crazy. I took them off and threw them out of the bus. I am quite blind without my glasses. I had no spare pairs, so I was virtually blind the whole time I was in Madagascar. Before we reached the last stop, one of the passengers who was an American and a Peace Corps volunteer, Randy, got off the bus. I got off with him. Randy started a conversation, and I went with him to a restaurant to meet his friend and to have something to eat. They both were very nice, and I didn't talk very much but did ask if they knew somewhere I could spend the night.

Randy helped me get a room at a motel. The "motel" consisted of tiny independent cabins that were triangular and made out of wood. Inside there was a table, chair, and single bed. Through an opening was a shower area with a bucket of water, soap, and cup. There was a hole in the ground that served as a toilet. It was simple and all that I needed. Thankfully, there were no mirrors.

Outside was the beach and beautiful ocean. I was afraid to even go into the ocean, which I love. I lay down on the beach, fully dressed and watched the surf. I slept that night, and the next day went looking for a boat that would take me to St. Marie Island. I walked back and forth past shacks on a hillside. My thoughts were that when the earthquake that was coming hit these homes, they would be destroyed by mudslides. I felt that there was light inside of me that could bless these homes and keep them safe just by walking by them. I spent a couple of hours doing this. Then I found the boat and had to have my passport checked. I met Randy again and he asked if I wanted to accompany him to the island where he was going as well. My intuition said don't trust him because his name is Randy. In Anglo-English, Randy means "horny." I sat at a small café and waited for the boat to go. A woman sat down beside me and had semi-precious unpolished stones for sale. I kept buying more and had to put them up to my eyes so I could see them. This protected me from those looking for me, for I believed again that the military was trying to find me. Finally the boat was ready to leave, and I climbed aboard.

As we pulled into St. Marie, there was a man, Naili, who met the boat and had a car to take people to his motel. I went with him. The motel was only about 15 minutes away, and Naili owned it. It was similar to the previous one but had toilets. It was right on the beach, which I loved, but the water was very shallow. Naili was kind. The second night there, he invited me to go dancing so we went. After some dancing, we were standing on the beach, and I could see a ship that I took to be a French warship. I was sure that they were searching for me, and a car drove by that I thought was full of the *gendarmes.*

Naili and I started kissing, and I had my back to the road. He then asked me to marry him. Having spent two months in Africa in the 1970s, I knew that his proposal translated to will you have sex with me. I told him that I would marry him, and we headed back to the motel. We had sex, and then I started acting like a wife as opposed to a tourist. I helped his mother in the kitchen and did small chores. Naili had seen the money I was carrying, and he put it into his car's trunk for safekeeping. I did not want to have sex again, so I took my things and walked down the beach. I saw a tree that was low enough to climb and almost hung out over the water. I climbed the tree and spent the day and night there. I thought that the tree was going to break off and float out to sea with me on it. Needless to say that did not happen. I walked into town several times on the hot, dusty, potholed road, and Naili came looking for me and brought me back to the motel. He saw to it that I ate at mealtimes, even though I only ate rice and fish. There was a cat with her kitten, and I fed the cat some of my fish.

I believed that there was going to be a tsunami that was going to destroy everything on the island except perhaps the Catholic Church that had been built on the highest land. I wanted to take a boat trip up the island, and I thought the tsunami would hit while we were in the boat. Naili arranged a boat trip after warning me that it would be expensive. We went on the trip and stopped at a fancier resort about a couple of hours away. We went in and had a drink. I was only drinking bottled water because I knew that other water was polluted. While I was up there, I gathered pieces of driftwood and stones and carried them back to the boat. They humored me, and let me keep them until we got back to Naili's motel.

Naili also took me inland to see a pretty waterfall and cut some coconuts. We rode on his motorcycle too. Unfortunately I could barely see anything without my glasses. I became afraid of Naili and didn't know where to go. I had been sure that the tsunami would hit and it didn't. I was confused by this just as I had been by so many directives before. However, I was still sure that the French military was after me and that I should not use toilets because they polluted the water.

TO BE JESUS

8/8/2005

To walk on earth
As he once did
Giving up everything
To save the earth
Living from compassion
for all beings
And complete trust
in the Universe
Only the trusted intuitions
were but my thoughts
and not of the me
I know
My thoughts wanted me blind
and mute
Physically punishing
To cross the dream threshold
So I live my fearful dreams
of running in foreign places
Each external encounter is imbued with meaning
LJ licenses – my initials: a sign of guardian angels
bird shit on car - a sign of disapproval
light reflections – Martians and helping stars
Avoiding mirrors – they could see me that way
Or did I know I would see another me there?
No voices, no hallucinations
but intuited directions
my conscious being gave up my free will
Was it another spirit or my own subconscious
that took me over?

One night there was a meeting about me, and because it was in French, I couldn't tell what they said. However, they put me in a car and drove me to the "hospital," two large rooms that looked like classrooms. I vomited on the way there. I understood that they said I had malaria. When we got to the hospital, they gave me an IV, and no one told me what was happening. I spent two days there, and looked to escape. A man who was there as a visitor or a patient, I'm not sure which, said to me, "you understand that you are Jesus Christ." I answered "yes." I believed that to mean that I was working to save the planet and the human species and that I may be killed for trying to do so. The self-aggrandizement that I felt, and that seems to come with schizophrenia, was due to the thought I had that the directives on how to act came directly from God, Source, Gaia, Great Spirit, Allah, or the Tao.

In the hospital, there were large insects on the walls. I couldn't see them well but they were larger than geckos, probably a foot in length. I believed that they were robots that the extraterrestrials sent to watch me. A man guarded me to make sure I didn't leave the room where they put me. While he was there, I shook his bed at night to wake him up. After several times of doing this, he left to find the doctor. I ran out of the hospital and hid in a ravine the rest of the night. I could feel the dirt and vines under me as I lay down upon the earth. I could hear the night animals and noises. Just before morning, I crawled out of the ravine and wandered through the town. As I walked past one woman, she screamed and ran inside her house. I must have looked pretty scary.

I saw another woman and walked up to her and asked her for some water. I had no purse, no money, no food or water; nothing with me. Aina gave me water and took me into her house. She spoke little English, and I spoke little French and none of the language of Madagascar. She gave me food and asked if I wanted a shower. I nodded yes. She ran a clothing store and gave me clean clothes. Her house had two sleeping areas. One was for her husband and self and younger son and the other bed for her elder son who was about seven. I stayed with her and her family for several days, sleeping in her older son's bed. She fed me and bought bottled water for me and totally accepted me. I couldn't believe her incredible kindness to a complete stranger. I was, and continue to be, so full of gratitude to her.

After a few days of living with Aina, she took me to the police chief along with a Peace Corps volunteer who spoke English and French and the local language. I was asked the name of my father, which I told them. I got back my small yoga mat bag with several clothes in it and my purse with most of the money gone. I didn't question the money. I was wondering how much money I should give to Aina but didn't ask the Peace Corps volunteer. I guessed, and I'm sure I didn't give her as much as I should have. The next day I went back to the police station and was told that I would be going home. Evidently the US Embassy had contacted my father, and he was paying for a medical evacuation. One of the policemen was going with me by plane to Antananarivo, the capital city. Meanwhile the Embassy had sent a nurse and a guy to travel with me. I shut down on the plane and kept my eyes closed the whole way, shutting out the world and all around me.

Once we got to a motel room, the nurse helped me bathe. My eyes were still shut. I didn't open them until later when the police and Embassy people, except for the nurse, had left. That night I didn't sleep all night. I had a light bulb from the lamp next to my bed, and I took the shade off. I put it under my bedcover and stared at the bulb as its image left an impression on my retina. As long as I could see the imprint of the filament, I felt safe. I was keeping the extraterrestrials away by staring at the light. That meant that when I needed to go to the bathroom I had to get to the toilet and back before the imprint on my retina left. So instead I urinated on the blanket that was on the side of the bed. The nurse, who was on the couch in the adjoining room, woke once to check on me, so I turned off the light for a few minutes. She then went back to sleep and I turned the light back on.

I met with a doctor from the Embassy who asked me questions the next day. The nurse kindly saw to it that my few pieces of clothing were washed. However, I believed there were substances in the soap that made my clothes unwearable. I then left Madagascar with a different person. She was a woman in her twenties who had never left Madagascar. It was a night flight to Paris. At one point I sat in the chair of a woman who had gone to the bathroom. She was angry that I took her chair, so I moved back to mine. When we arrived at Charles de Gaulle airport, I was hungry. We had eaten the packet of cookies and some of the candies that the guy from the Embassy gave us. We sat and waited at the arrival gate all day. Several times I tried to walk away, but my companion asked me to please not leave. She was very sincere and caring and, I think, somewhat frightened by the size of the airport. Meanwhile, the man who was supposed to meet us to take me home was waiting at the departure gate for our flight. We finally went to the departure gate, and I left Paris traveling first class with the medical evacuation guy. We were served food, which I ate with my hand. I figured if I was in first class I could eat any way I wanted to. I also changed my clothes and then remembered that they were washed in a powder that I thought would make me itch, so I changed back again.

We arrived in Atlanta, and I told the med evac guy that I wanted to see my stepson who lived there. He said "no," that he was taking me to Washington, DC. I was expecting a hero's welcome in California where my friends and family would come and congratulate me on saving the world from the extraterrestrials. As he was checking in for our next flight, I walked away and out of the airport. I had my small yoga bag of clothes and my purse with some vanilla beans, semi-precious stones, and 25,000 Franc Malgache, the Madagascar currency equivalent to about six US dollars. I rode one of the buses to a local motel and went inside. I realized I had no US money, so I left.

I walked to the back of the motel and into a little wood where I buried some clothes. The rest of my clothes except for what I was wearing I left under the trees. I then walked not knowing where I was going. I saw two large bushes and managed to climb under one of them. It was a thick bush at the side of an industrial park building. There I took off my clothes and tried to bury myself in the dirt. I thought that the head of the extraterrestials I had met in Saint Marie was flying into Atlanta to talk to our military. I was afraid they would find me.

After spending several hours under the bush, I got dressed again and walked out to find a motel. There was a fountain outside a motel so

I washed my hair in the fountain. I then walked into the motel and asked if I could use their phone to call my stepson. They let me use the phone. I first called my former partner to get my stepson's telephone number. It was about 3:00 in the morning. She gave me his number and talked to the motel person. Shortly thereafter a policeman appeared and asked me for my social security number and other personal details. I was listed as a missing person. I was taken to the police station, and they called my stepson. He then came to pick me up.

When we got to my stepson's house, I was in a complete panic that the extraterrestrials had followed me there. I sat in the living room with my stepson and told him that an extraterrestrial was eating me from the inside of my stomach out. I was nearly hysterical as I recounted this. After awhile my feelings subsided and I was exhausted. I asked my stepson to tie me up so that if I changed into an extraterrestrial I wouldn't hurt anyone. He tied my hands and feet together with a bathrobe tie and helped me into bed. I slept for a few hours. Then I woke up and had a shower. The power of the extraterrestrials had abated but I still felt that I was unsafe. I crouched on the kitchen floor with a cup of tea but said very little. My stepson said that my son was coming to pick me up and that his flight from DC would land shortly. In the meantime, my stepson had arranged to get my passport and ticket back from the med evac guy who actually lived in Atlanta.

My son arrived, and we climbed aboard the next plane for DC. As the plane took off I turned my head up, down, and around taking the laser shots that the extraterrestrials were using to shoot the plane down. I was saving the plane from their bombardment. I was sure my son would be proud of me, but I didn't tell him what I was doing. He asked me to please stop, and once we were out of range I did so. My welcoming homecoming was a trip straight to North Arundel Hospital, where they put me under observation. They gave me medication, and I spent the day shuffling around the room. My son stayed with me the whole time, and I was very grateful for that. I could feel his love and compassion for me, his deep caring.

The next day they transferred me to Sheppard and Enoch Pratt Hospital. I was brought in on a stretcher to the most disturbed ward. Although I would write, I didn't speak for almost two weeks. I felt like the staff and doctors really wanted to help me, but I also sensed that extraterrestrials were listening to me and to any word I said. I didn't take my medication, unbeknownst to the nurses and doctors. They had activities that I participated in, and I went outdoors on the deck whenever the smokers could go out. I don't smoke, but I loved being outdoors, even as it got colder. I didn't have any glasses or contacts so it was difficult to do some things. My son came to visit often, as did my former partner. Her son was in town from North Carolina and he came to see me. We talked about how I could get more physical exercise. I didn't have the discipline to do my own exercises but I felt the need for it. The hospital didn't offer any exercise programs or equipment.

During this time, I was afraid of my roommate and spent the night in the seclusion room on the floor instead of in my bed. I was then able to change rooms. My former partner gave me a small stuffed cat, which I thought had poison on it. I put it in the washing machine and dryer before I would sleep with it and carry it around. It provided some solace to me in this lonely world. I refused to see her. I had strong negative feelings towards her that she did not deserve. I started talking for the first time since my arrival when I was brought before a judge who was going to decide my fate. They were talking about sending me somewhere for a longer period of time and giving guardianship of me to my former partner. As a result, I started talking. I didn't tell them that the lights I could see through the windows represented friendly stars to me that were watching over me or that I believed extraterrestrials could hear me if I spoke. I answered the judge's questions in a sane way, and he decided that a guardianship was not necessary.

I was able to function living in my two realities even though I felt afraid and also guided by the Universe. Several times I was permitted to visit another ward. People here were considered to be much more functional, and there were more activities and programs for them. Here were the people who had tried to commit suicide or who were changing their medications, or were depressed, or even a few that had bipolar disorder. However, the majority of time was on my own ward, where more disturbed patients were located. My daughter said that I could come live with her and her new husband. I was deeply touched by her offer but didn't want to disturb the newlyweds. My son told me that he was in favor of my former partner gaining guardianship over me and my finances. I was very hurt and angry at this, particularly since I had such negative feelings towards her. I didn't know what I would do once I got out of the hospital, but my full concentration was on how to get out. I signed a statement that the doctors could no longer talk to my son and former partner about me. I had hit the magic button. Two days later I was released from the hospital. My doctor gave me a shot of prolixin deconate right before I left. I had no one to pick me up at the hospital, so I was given money to take a cab to the train station, ride the train to DC, and take the bus home. However, I wasn't given enough money to make it to the train station. Fortunately the taxi driver said it was okay.

At Union Station in DC, I perused the railway schedules, and I'm sure that if I had had any money I would have taken a train somewhere and right back into a psychotic event. Instead I took the subway to Silver Spring, MD, and walked to where I used to work. I spent the afternoon there waiting until a friend of mine was finished with her work. Then she gave me a ride home. I was very grateful to her, particularly when I found out later that the only bus that would take me home left me with a mile to walk. I was on the border of slipping again into a psychotic state but the shot of prolixin deconate kept my other realities from creeping back in. I knew for the first time that I had created a reality with extraterrestrials, spies, and poisonings that was not real. That realization saved my life. I was left with confusion and fear but sought to do things that would help support me physically, mentally, spiritually, and emotionally. For the first time, I was willing to take my medication, even though the side effects were serious and caused Parkinsonian symptoms.

IN MEMORY

8/5/05

Stut tered   Stut terred
Move ment   break ing
Tongue push ing
Swol len on teeth
Push ing for ward
Bod y re sis ting
Gait shuff ling
Feet for got ten
how to walk
Mouth for got ten
how to talk
Show er ing
What comes next?
Raised Hands
re mem ber not
E very motion
Re quires thought
The mind dis con nects
Sy nap ses mis fire
Nerves gy rate
A hun dred shat tered
mirror shards
Reflect me now

A journal entry on November 16, 2004, written 12 days after my release from Sheppard and Enoch Pratt Hospital is included below.

Out of Sheppard Pratt hospital Nov. 4 on prolixin decoanate – a shot. Added seroquel 25 mg. 11/11 and had another shot of prolixin on Friday 11/12/04. Saturday my friend did a shamanic cleansing of my house, and it feels better. I talked to my friend, Edwin, on Sunday for three hours. Thoughts of suicide, difficult to reconcile what has happened to me and where do I go from here. Yoga this morning and went for a walk in the woods after a haircut and went to a group sponsored by NAMI [National Alliance for the Mentally Ill]. Things are so hard at least that is what my thoughts tell me. I felt totally overwhelmed talking about how to apply for SSD benefits. I'm on the edge it seems. My thoughts are talking most of the time telling me how impossible everything is. I've called and am going to volunteer time at the church office and teach chakra ta'i chi at a senior living center. My mind says can I do it? I get tired of hearing my mind lead with fear and anxiety all the time. How not to listen to it? It seems with the medication that this is what I have to deal with – constant negativity, fear, terror, thoughts that I can't do things. I feel that I can't make it in life and without the medications I go into incredible delusions that take over my body, mind and soul. Great alternatives! I'm scared about money and can't think of the future without feeling petrified. I'm tired and my energy is low. Going to Teresa's house tonight for shamanic journeying – hope that helps. I don't feel OK and I don't know what to do. I'm trying to talk to reach out, my mouth feels shaky. I don't know what someone could do for me. Give me help with SSD benefits – dare I ask my former partner? After all I've put her through. I feel like my life is meaningless now – who am I relating to?

Relationships are mutually beneficial – are mine with Teresa, Edwin, the kids. How to get me back – is that even possible? What do I have to offer, to give, to life, to myself, to others? From where I am, things look pretty bleak. Yet, I was on the verge of suicide in my twenties and swore never again. I love my body. I don't want to hurt it. I can still see the beauty – the buck with four points, the four deer, and the twigs with spider's web strands sparkling in the sun. There is beauty – I wish I had my poem – I walk in beauty before me, behind me, all around me. Universe help me. I want to open, to live, to be and then I think this is probably as good as it gets. Not to be shot full of medication so I don't know whether it is day or night, no memory, locked inside four walls without a breath of fresh air for days or weeks. No exercise, nothing to do except vegetate and be in pain and wish I was dead. No, I'm much better than that now and what is my future? I don't feel I can take care of myself - but I am. I'm fixing meals, doing bills, taking out garbage, existing. I am driving places, doing things, taking walks. Be easy on yourself, little bird – how can you say that to me – the voice that led me to Madagascar, betrayed me – where is my God now? Where is the Universe? Where is my beloved, the divine light? That who would hurt me, all I wanted to do was to live in the moment, be in alignment with the Universe and do its will and I have become a schizophrenic crackpot instead who can not even take care of myself much less do anything with my life. I'm crying as I write these words. What is the truth about me. All of it was delusion? What about the intuition? What brought me back from Madagascar? What did I learn – was any of it real?

I've learned not to drive cars, not to poison the earth with toxic chemicals and radiation. Not to pee or crap into water. I have learned to be with nature as much as possible, to be part of it. We are not the highest, most conscious species. I think we are probably the lowest and we have choice. I want to choose unconditional love or compassion and it seems I keep choosing fear. I forget I have a choice – don't we all. To sing, dance, drum, listen, love, have compassion for myself and others. We have a choice to live in the moment, letting go of the past and future. Yet is that delusional for I am losing or have lost everything? What is security? I was OK with nothing, I trusted without fear and came back. Now I can't sustain that – I just live in the fear and I'm sick of it. I've spent money so unwisely and now I'm afraid that I will end up a beggar on the street. Maybe that is what I am to learn next. I gave up everything and now I am back, I have it back at least some of it, parts of my old life. What is happening with my former partner? What is happening with me? I grasp for her like clutching at lost straws wanting to find myself – not much of a relationship. I am afraid – again and again – for me I need to sit with my fear and accept it. I'm running to others to make sense of what has happened to me and they can not do that for me. It is as though I am apart from myself, watching Mr. Bojangles dance. Maybe Madagascar was my soul purpose and now what – you keep living and see. The Universe is not dead or gone. It is so difficult to get out of bed in the morning.

I was not taking any benzotropine to counter the effects of the prolixin deconate, and I found myself with Parkinsonian symptoms, otherwise known as tardive dyskenesia. I shook, and my tongue pushed hard against my upper palate and teeth. My fine motor skills were gone, and it was difficult to write or sign papers because of the shaking. It scared me. It also took enormous concentration to do simple tasks. When taking a shower and getting out, I had to focus on each movement to do it. I started seeing a holistic psychiatrist who believed in muscle testing and energy medicine. She changed my medicine to abilify at a very low dosage. This stopped the shaking and tardive dyskenesia symptoms.

In November 2004 after my fourth hospitalization, I finally realized that I had a mental disorder and that I was living in two separate realities. I had not taken the medication given to me so the psychiatrist gave me a shot of medication, prolixin, and released me. I followed my discharge plan of seeing a psychiatrist and taking medication, but I could barely make it in the world.

I felt as though the Universe had let me down, especially when I sacrificed so much. After spending almost two years alone looking for some reason as to why I was having psychotic episodes, I focused on becoming a part of communities. I decided to set up a schedule that would involve interacting with people and getting exercise, even though my movements were tight and rigid and I spoke very little. I joined Paint Branch Unitarian Universalist church and reached out to people, starting new friendships. I went swimming, joined a seniors' arthritis group at the pool, took the beginning course of Anusara yoga, joined a drumming group, danced in a dancer's group at church, acted as a receptionist at a yoga center and church. I started attending weekly gatherings of the Insight Meditation Community of Washington. There I meditated for half an hour and listened to a talk on Buddhist psychology and its application in the world. I felt lost, full of fear, and isolated most of that year but slowly developed friendships. I spoke with the Minister at church about my journey with my illness and he was very empathic and yet could not help me through my fear. Slowly, as I became more physically strong, I also learned to work with my mental states and participate more in group activities.

Meditation has not come easy to me. At first I couldn't sit still long enough to meditate. So I practiced ta'i chi chuan, which is meditative movement. It involves focusing on each movement so that the mind is concentrating on one thing, the action. I started practicing this in 1993 and did it everyday at lunchtime. It brought a peace and calmness that I cherish. I still could not do sitting meditation until about 1997. Prior to that time as soon as I sat down I thought of all the things that I needed to do so I got up and did them. I thought that meditation meant clearing the mind so I would have no thoughts. After years I realized that the thoughts still come, but now there is an awareness beyond those thoughts, and I can stay seated and just notice them. For the past four years I have meditated most days for at least 30 minutes. This was true even while I was in hospitals or having a psychotic episode. There was a greater awareness but even stronger fear-based thoughts or directives that I couldn't shake.

While on medication, especially the mood stabilizing drug depakote, I am deprived of feeling my body sensations or any emotions, such as sadness, joy, or anger. Without these emotions in my relationships, I don't know what I'm feeling or where my personal boundaries are. I don't fully experience the euphoria of being in love with my partner or the joy that is brought to me by my grandchildren. Only twice in this past year have I had tears come to my eyes or felt like crying. Before the kidney surgery, I'd feel teary at least several times a month. I have also lost my sexual libido. Further, I feel that my creativity is more difficult to access. Fortunately, I still have my poetry. I used to write poems to express my feelings; since the kidney surgery, I write to be more aware of what my feelings are. I have difficulty accessing a lot of my feelings until I can see them on paper through my poetry.

Sadly, fear, while dampened, is still the strongest emotion I feel. At times I have lived in two realities: one filled with delusions and catastrophic fear, and the other a "normal" way of seeing and acting in the world. I've asked myself the questions of "Who am I?," "Who is the observer?," "Who is telling me how to act?," and "Why do I believe my thoughts and act on them?" It has been very difficult for me to tell whether the Universe is speaking to me or whether the directives I have been given are from my own convoluted mind. One thing that has helped me to differentiate is to look at the outcome of the directed actions. If the actions are harmful to me or to others, they are not from the Universe. When I am in a manic state it is almost impossible for me to recognize that what I am doing is not from the Universe.

I realize that the medication is to help control the fear and to make my behavior more acceptable to society. I would, however, like others to realize what significant things I'm giving up, particularly in terms of my feelings. This loss of being able to fully experience life is one of the biggest reasons that I might go off the medication (see the "Why I Stopped Taking Medications" section in the *Appendix*).

Because the medication has robbed me of direct access to emotions, I have had to find a back door to my feelings. That doorway is the body, which never lies. Meditation and acupressure and, to a lesser extent, shamanism, give me direct access to what my body is feeling and, with it, the accompanying emotions. I have become more aware of what's happening physically and of what is represents to me spiritually, emotionally, physically, and mentally. A sudden coughing spell, for example, often means that I have feelings around what's being said in a conversation and I'm having difficulty saying something I need to say. I previously would have disregarded such somatic sensations. I now pause to look for what I'm feeling before I speak or act. I have learned to hold myself with a greater awareness as I try to balance the medication with my daily life.

MEDITATION

7/3/09

Sitting
Sinking
Loving-kindness prayer
Interrupted
Phone rings
Cat meows
Doing thoughts
Stick
and pull
Me
Out of all sounds
A wholeness
Watching
What mind tricks
Play

Vipassana meditation, a form of Buddhist practice, also gives me a way to access what is going on in my body. It involves scanning the body and focusing on the areas of pain, discomfort, or tingling. By simply breathing and observing the breath or noticing the sounds around me, I can bring my mind back from its many thoughts and accompanying emotions and let go, resting again in a spaciousness. An observer appears, which is an awareness that calls the mind back. When emotions are strong, there is usually a story connected to them. I drop the story and find the emotion(s) in my body where they appear as sensation(s). Then I can focus on the sensation(s) and feel that energy move in my body and out of it. The pain or sensation is not always released, but I find that there is a distance from it. I am no longer identified as the pain but rather the awareness or consciousness that holds the pain. A shift in perspective occurs, and often information comes forth from that pain.

I have been on two five-day meditation retreats with the Insight Meditation Community of Washington and numerous day longs and weekend retreats since 1997. Each time I have selected an aspiration or intention for the retreat. For the weekend retreat in January 2009, my intention was to know what gifts I have to give to the world. The format of the retreat was to have dinner Friday night and a talk by one of the teachers and instructions for the retreat. Saturday began at 6:00 a.m. and alternated sitting and walking meditation during the day with time for three meals.

The retreat was silent except for an hour when we met in small groups with one of the three teachers and talked of our experience or difficulties in meditating. I believe that the silence and compassion held by the teachers and the participants for each other allowed very deep sharing. An important insight I gained was that asking to know what gifts I have negates the gifts that I am already sharing. It also reflects my belief that I do not have a birthright to live unless I am doing something that is worthwhile, like saving the earth. This was a recurring theme in my psychotic episodes.

Over the past ten years, I have realized more and more that "being" is much more important than "doing." I define being as my presence, the compassion I hold for myself and others. Both Sri Sri Ravi Shankar, a spiritual master from India, and Mother Theresa possess a tremendous "being." I am sure there are others as well, but these are two individuals that I have personally seen and been with for a short period of time. In the sharing of that Vipassana meditation retreat circle, I expressed how I had sought purpose for my life, especially since 2003, and how several times I had doubted continuing my existence if I did not have purpose or connection to the Universe. This retreat was a safe place to express these deep thoughts. After the group, we returned to silence. There was another talk in the evening, then some chanting, and bedtime around 10:00 p.m. Sunday there was more meditation and a closing ceremony.

A key tenet in Buddhist psychology, Vipassana meditation, and Process Acupressure is that the mind is not to be trusted. The mind conjures up thoughts, which is just what minds do. It doesn't mean that we have to believe in or act on those thoughts. Buddhist practices help to train the mind and help to differentiate the directives of the mind from the observer that is detached from the mind. It is a process, however, and not one that happens overnight.

With time and through my experiences, I have learned to distrust my thoughts. My mind lies to me. My guidepost is whether the thoughts are fear-based or not. When I believe that the person taking my blood in the hospital is an extraterrestrial, the belief is based on fear. I do not know from where this thought comes, but I do not have to believe it or act on it. My thoughts build constructs, ways of perceiving the world. I am here to save the world, so there must be a duality of those who are here to destroy it. For me, each one of us has made choices and taken actions out of ignorance that harm the earth and its creatures. There are those who also intentionally pollute the environment, create war, and destroy its beauty. They project their internal hatred, fear, anger, cravings, and doubts upon the world. In my psychotic episodes, extraterrestrials inhabit those latter people. They are chasing me and those that I love in order to kill us. I am projecting my fears onto the world and people around me. At the same time during these episodes,

I know intuitively who I can trust, and I believe that I am protected by higher beings or loving spirits.

From my perspective now, I do believe that everything I experience provides me with an opportunity to spiritually awaken. This includes everything, whether it is labeled "good" or "bad" at any given time. It is even true of the schizophrenia I experience and my psychotic episodes. I am not a schizo-affective person. I have a schizo-affective disorder. The difference between these statements is highly significant. My disorder does not define who I am.

In January 2005, I took on some volunteer work at church. I had joined this church in January 2004, and it felt good to be accepted into a community. The volunteer work in the office was difficult for me, even though the tasks were very easy. I was afraid to answer the phone or to act on my own initiative. My memory was poor, and I often didn't understand what was wanted or expected of me. I didn't understand why my memory was poor and can only guess that new neural pathways were rebuilding themselves. However, the people in the office and the administrator were very supportive and caring.

I saw my holistic psychiatrist for a couple of months much to the consternation of my former partner, and my son. Finally, on their advice, I changed to a psychiatrist who operated in more traditional ways. I also took a battery of tests that showed my non-functionality. My former partner helped me to apply for disability through the Social Security Administration, which I did receive. That would not have happened without her help.

TO HEAL

5/14/05

To heal
To become whole again
Shattered chards mending
Thoughts full untangling
Clutching ivy
Torn from the bark
hanging disconnected
Flailing against wind
Being brought together
Wounds bound with silken thread
Gossamer strength
black spider spun
The world is one
Splintered fragments
gathered into
sticky web
where each strand
holds meaning
and being
within the universe

In June 2005, I changed psychiatrists again and started seeing a licensed social worker, Lori, for weekly "talk" sessions. The sessions with Lori were incredibly valuable to me. We worked together with different techniques. I felt that I could say anything to her and that there would be no judgment, just compassion. My psychiatrist I saw for medication. Both of them were connected with a Sheppard and Enoch Pratt outpatient clinic. It was a slow battle to regain my physical and mental health. I took a class for seniors with arthritis at a nearby pool and gradually started swimming laps again.

In August, on the spur of the moment, I signed up for a shiatsu program that was given at a local massage school. It consisted of 795 hours of anatomy, physiology, and practice sessions. I didn't know if I could think or retain information or succeed at all. My affect was still very flat, and I had difficulties establishing relationships even though my classmates were very accepting. I was part of a community and had class Monday through Thursday evenings, which helped me tremendously. It gave me purpose, stimulated my mind, and gave me a community to be part of. I attended these classes until February 2007, when I graduated with a 4.0, 100% average.

THOUGHTS

9/9/06

Sitting
staring
not knowing
what to do next
Staying in the moment
Afraid of thoughts
that pop up
The old fears
still scare me
See the bird
feel the breeze
on my skin
What is next?
Indecision
Afraid to just be
to just sit
Afraid of what?
the jumble of thoughts?
They are only thoughts
to be dismissed

At the end of February 2007, I went to visit my parents in Houston, Texas. My mother had broken her leg New Year's Eve and was living in an assisted living center that I had arranged for her. During the visit, she wanted me to clean out her house and get it ready for sale. I was totally overwhelmed by the job, but no one else was willing to take it on. I was able to clear the house and get a contractor to make the house ready for sale. As I was working on the house, I felt that the Universe was working with me again and making things possible. Things went smoothly.

I started seeing signs that were personalized. I was driving over to the house one morning, and an ambulance passed me. My thought was not to visit the house but to go see my mother first and go to the house later. Otherwise I might end up in the ambulance. My mother had been living alone in this house since her second husband died fifteen years ago. The whole time she was there, she complained that someone was getting into the house and wearing her clothes, spilling fuel oil on the carpet, cutting the back to the lounge chair, etc. She had changed the locks many times and the house was very secure. Even the windows were nailed shut. I had dismissed her talk. However, while I was in Houston someone had pulled the wallpaper off the wall of one of the bathrooms and then had taken a drawer from the family room cabinets. Only my brother and mother supposedly had keys. I changed the locks again so that only the realtor and I had a key, and the incidents stopped. To this day I do not know who was doing these things or why.

I was functioning well but was very tired. I extended my stay by several days so I could finish up with the house. I started sleeping poorly and became manic. I called my counselor to ask if I should increase my medication. She said "no" and advised me to take benadryl to sleep. I didn't talk to my psychiatrist. Instead I quit taking my medication for two days. The first day was by accident, and the second day was perhaps because I was feeling good. On my way home, I drove right by the airport and missed my flight. Fortunately I caught another flight that was right after the first.

I called my son to let him know I would be late. He was picking me up at the airport. I arrived back Monday, March 5, and saw my counselor on March 6. I was already on the slippery slope, but none of us knew it. I had mailed boxes of silver and china that my Mother had given to me back to my house from Houston. My son helped me store them in the basement. I had planned to go to the beach with my boyfriend on Wednesday. Instead, when he arrived, I told him I was going to the beach by myself and asked him to help load the boxes (of silver and china) from the basement into my car. I was not speaking to anyone but just writing notes. By this time, I thought that the extraterrestrials were tracking me again and that they could find me through the silver and china. It was important to get rid of them and to get rid of all pictures. They could track me and family members through photographs. I rushed through the house gathering pictures and, with my car loaded with the boxes of silver and china, I left the house.

My intention was to get rid of everything, but I thought the car would be tracked, so I parked it at a Honda dealer's lot and walked to a strip mall close by. I bought a pair of jeans to put over the pants I had on and a new shirt, too, so that those who were chasing me would have the wrong description. I then took a cab to metro and from there to Reagan National Airport. I went up to the boarding pass machines and typed in my name on several different machines. It didn't give me a pass. I left the airport and went across the street to the Hilton.

By this time I thought that the extraterrestrials inhabiting human bodies were meeting at the Hilton. It was 11:00 p.m. or so. I knew that I was supposed to spend the night at the Hilton so that my presence there would keep them from taking over the earth. I spent about $300 for a room and then slept for about three hours. I got up and sang "Spirit of Life" and left my new pair of blue jeans with a note that said, "if you need these, please take them." I left the hotel down the back stairs and walked over to an adjoining motel. I asked them if I could wait in their lobby, which they let me do. Because I quit wearing a watch five years ago, I wasn't sure of the time, but thought it to be about 3:00 or 4:00 a.m.

I took my little suitcase and rolled it through underground Crystal City. It was relatively warm and no one was there. I stopped at a little table and fell asleep for an hour or so. By this time the metro was open, and I got on it and rode around for several hours. I finally got off at Silver Spring and took a bus a few blocks from the station. The bus driver kindly let me on without paying. The smallest bill I had was $20. I then walked to a friend's house where a meditation session was scheduled with a group of my friends.

I arrived early and wrote a note saying that I was not speaking, a vow of silence. I also proceeded to write out a list of people with names and numbers and asked Lois to call them when I had gone. Once the group arrived for our loving-kindness meditation, I warned them of the water contamination and the extraterrestrials. I was so sure of what I was saying. They realized I needed help and told me so. At that point I got up and walked out of the house, leaving my coat behind when they tried to stop me. I hid behind bushes and houses as my friends looked for me.

I was able to escape and take a bus back to the metro station and then on to Crystal City. I ate some lunch in Crystal City and walked again back and forth in the mall under the buildings. A lot of young, busy people were all on their way somewhere. I bought a hat and a shawl and then an attaché case and gloves. I kept walking back and forth and finally headed for the airport. I walked up to the boarding pass machines I had played with the previous night and entered my name. This time I got a boarding pass and it was to Chicago. I sat down and waited for my flight. It seemed that the "important people" were on this flight with their attaché cases. I got up, and they processed my boarding pass before they realized I was on the next flight. I sat down again and waited. Right before boarding my flight I thought that I had to leave my new attaché case full of gloves and hat there, which I did. I felt afraid but without realizing why. I got on the plane and we took off for Chicago.

On the way there I sat in the wrong seat, but they didn't make me move. The young man next to me was very pleasant and sorted things out. At first I liked him; then I felt that he was controlling me, and I became fearful of him. My mind started thinking highly complex thoughts, like 3-dimensional chess or like a computer crashing because it's overloaded by too much data. I couldn't keep the ideas straight.

Lynn Johnson

My thoughts were racing. I was exhausted but couldn't sleep. As I was getting off the plane, the stewardess looked at me and asked if I was okay. I told her that no, I wasn't okay. She asked me to stand to the side until other passengers got off and then asked me again what she could do for me. I told her I needed to call my son in Maryland. I gave her his number, and she placed the call for me. My son talked to another attendant, and he explained that I was a missing person who suffers from a schizo-affective disorder. The attendant arranged for me to take the next plane out back to BWI, where my son would meet me.

I was escorted to a room with a policeman. I slept on several chairs pushed together until my flight. My son had permission to come through security to pick me up. He told me he would take me somewhere that was safe. I told him where my car was and what was in it and why. He had been tracking me through my credit card expenditures and was one step behind me. I felt nothing but love from him, even though I was once again in a psychotic episode. He took me to Montgomery General Hospital, and they admitted me the next day. He spent all night with me until they took me upstairs.

GODDESS

3/13/07

Her love is never gone
Here in the early dawn
Things are so bleak and unknown
Yet now there is a streak of light
To guide us through the darkest night
And open our hearts by breaking them
And grow our soul wisdom
So laugh through the tears
It will not be many years
Until as one
We join the sun

March 9-20, 2007, I was in the hospital. What a difference! Immediately I noticed that the staff was nice, receptive, smiling, and joked with one another. I didn't feel the overarching fear and anger that I had felt at Washington Adventist. Sheppard Pratt was a good place, but Montgomery General was better by far. There was always someone who would listen to what you said, and I did talk there. The doctors increased the abilify dosage and then changed me over to risperdal and dekonate. I didn't feel like a zombie, and my delusions began to evaporate. I still believed that the tap water was contaminated and that extraterrestrials were on the ward. I told my son this, and he got several water-testing kits. He tested his water at home and said that it was okay. I asked him to bring me jugs of purified water and then distilled water, which he did. The man who took blood and one of the patients appeared to me to be extraterrestrials and I was told that I could ask for someone else to take my blood. This acknowledgement, listening, and understanding made me feel much better and less isolated.

The first couple of nights I felt that the extraterrestrials were sending their lasers into the hospital and trying to kill me. The nurses let me sleep in the seclusion room next to the nurses' station. I found this reassuring. There were activities all day, including an exercise time and art therapy. I made two collages. The first showed my world view with extraterrestrials coming to take over the earth and people turning into extraterrestrials as their anger and hatred grew for one another. The second collage showed me in the center; the one that would save the world. Slowly my world of extraterrestrials, environmental catastrophes, and contaminated water retreated back into the recesses of my mind. Good friends visited me, and my son was always there. When these last delusional vestiges were gone, I was released.

I continued outpatient therapy for three weeks, which was helpful. Then I resumed my daily activities and joined a therapy group in May 2007 that I'm still attending. I changed psychiatrists to George Saiger M.D., who also facilitates a group of seven people. Participants in this group are asked to share what they are feeling while in the group. In August

2007, my therapist, Lori, left her job. I was very sad that I couldn't see her any more. I felt that she had always accepted me and extended her willingness to be there for me over the two years I had seen her. I cried for the first time in two years when she told me I wouldn't be able to continue seeing her. In August, I began seeing Dr. Saiger on a weekly basis and then every other week. His sessions are 50 minutes, and I feel a real sense of caring and honesty with him. He works with me and is not supercilious towards me or to the group members. He respects us as individuals and is very compassionate towards us. His group has been supportive and a place where I can share issues, particularly those associated with mental illness.

TRUE BELIEVER

4/19/07

What is true?
Where does it lie
amidst my jumbled thoughts?
Once more I reach out to save the world
and find extraterrestrials
and fear lurking
inside of me
and in projections on others
What is deeply felt
bubbles up
and once more I am running
Running from myself
or the enjoyment of the chase?
My dreams have crossed over
into daily reality
Perhaps night and day have exchanged for me
How can I slip between fingers of time
Slip through the net
concocted in surveillance
yet only of my son and friends
not the military, intelligence, or aliens
Why do I believe absolutely?
Where is the questioning?
It all collapses when I can no longer hold
each thought in my head
My intelligence is so miniscule
compared to universal intelligence
Is that why I believe?
And what do I believe in?
Is there a duality beyond the brain?
I choose to believe in the oneness
wholeness
not the duality of good and evil
Yet where do these thoughts come from?

What have I learned? Perhaps the biggest thing I've learned is to not believe my thoughts. I intellectually know that, and I am hoping that I can now live that and question my thoughts. If you can't trust your thoughts, what can you trust? If my thoughts lead me to actions that punish my body, I need to stop. I believe that my body never lies. My experiences have grown my compassion for myself, the mentally ill, the homeless, and for everyone. There does not appear to be a way to control my thoughts that lead to manic behavior and a psychotic break without medication. However, by being aware of these thoughts if and as they arise, I may be able to increase the medication at the time so that I do not descend the slippery slope.

Eckhart Tolle, in *A New Earth*, defines paranoid schizophrenia as a "fictitious story the mind has invented to make sense of a persistent underlying feeling of fear. The main element of the story is the belief that certain people (sometimes large numbers or almost everyone) are plotting against me, or are conspiring to control or kill me." [18] He also says that another characteristic is that of thinking that I am the center of the Universe and that I have the power to save the world. All of these statements ring true for me.

I believe, like Tolle, that all people have these feelings to a greater or lesser extent. For me these thoughts materialized and led to my "crazy" actions. Where did this all consuming, existential fear come from? I still do not know. I think that the medications I am taking, a mood stabilizer and an anti-psychotic, dampen my feelings and reduce the fear. The problem is they also reduce all emotions including joy. Without feelings, it is difficult to navigate this world.

My psychiatrist has recently reduced the level of the anti-psychotic, and I notice a shift in my ability to feel. Twice last week, I actually got angry, which helped me to know that I felt my boundaries were being violated. I could look at the situation in a different way and, after acknowledging my feelings to myself, respond in an appropriate way. Before 2003 I had always had strong feelings, even though in my family of origin feelings were never acknowledged or processed. I have struggled most of my life to be aware of my feelings and to feel them in my body.

I have spent a lifetime's journey of searching for purpose in my life and relationship with the Universe and the environment and people around me. When I was fourteen, I was sitting outside in my backyard under a tree reading a book. It was the *Silver Chalice* by Thomas Costain.[19] The book quoted the verse from *The Bible*, Matthew 6:25-34. It was telling me that I could live life without worrying about where my next meal would come from or how I would be given shelter or clothes. I reflected back to the summer camp and the minister there who seemed to live like that, but I couldn't think of anyone else who did or would even try it. I pondered this passage and then offered up the prayer that if this passage was really true that I be given a sign.

Within a minute, a lightning bolt hit the tree about twenty feet from mine. I could feel the energy traveling through the ground and up the tree I was leaning against. It catapulted me across the yard through a series of forward rolls. There wasn't a cloud in the sky. I was alright but thoroughly shaken. I didn't know what to do with the answer. It certainly seemed a sign, but it also seemed totally impractical to live this way. Imagine my delight and surprise some forty years later when reading Eckhart Tolle's book, *The Power of Now,* that Eckhart defined this passage as living in the present moment, not living irresponsibly. Living in the now is the key to spiritual living. The past or future does not exist, only the present moment does. There are times when one needs to plan, but the attention should be given to those steps or choices that one can make right here and now. Those choices help to determine our future.

FEELING HELD

10/3/06

Feeling held
whole
one with the Universe
all that is
one with all life
with the earth
no loneliness
no grasping
no clinging
to another
A sense of completeness
as I am
for who I am
surrounded in love
white light
It is always here
if I can only remember

In November 2004, I felt abandoned and betrayed by the Universe. How and why was I struck with mental illness and these psychotic episodes? I struggled to find my life's purpose and regain my physical, mental, emotional, and spiritual health. Gradually over a two-year period, I realized that it was the Universe that was with me, protecting me, and that I was acting from fear and "voices." I believe that there is purpose in learning life's lessons. I do not belittle the power of medication now, yet I am working with my psychiatrist to reduce the amount of medications as far as possible. I have come back to the Universe, the white light, and love and compassion.

My spiritual journey began around age ten, when I accepted Christ as my Savior. I went to a fundamentalist Christian Presbyterian camp. I felt love from the staff, counselors, and ministers that resonated with my own heart. I gave my testimonial of acceptance of Jesus and felt accepted. It helped that I also won "Camper of the Year" award. We had Bible readings everyday and passages to memorize. My paternal grandmother, an ardent Southern Baptist, would have been pleased. At fourteen, I realized when I went to fill out an application to be a Counselor in Training at this camp that I no longer believed in the prescribed doctrine. I did believe that we should all live like Jesus, but I did not believe he was God, or even that a patriarchal God existed. I started my questioning, which resulted in almost being killed by a lightning bolt. During my teenage years, I attended the Dutch Reformed Church, where I taught Sunday School. I became increasingly disillusioned with this church. What they talked about on Sunday was not how most members lived their lives. It didn't help that this church supported apartheid in South Africa.

By 17, I renounced Christianity and any institutional religion. At 17, I went to college and was exposed to philosophy for the first time. I loved using logic to prove things and even wrote one paper on the non-existence of God. I had so many questions like "Who am I?," "What or Who is God?," and "What is my purpose here on earth?" My logical constructs were not enough to give me answers. So I decided to pray, asking that I could live life fully and in that living find answers to these bigger questions. You would think that after my episode with the lightning I would be a little more careful in what I ask for.

When I was 36, I joined the Unitarian Universalist Church. I was looking for a spiritual community in which my children could learn about world religions and develop a bond with other children. Although my two children did not stick with the church past their teenage years, both of them have adopted similar values and principles to those listed below. Since 1986, I have attended Unitarian Universalist Churches and have been part of these communities. I am a spiritual seeker and have enjoyed being in the company of other spiritual seekers who have the same core principles:

1) the inherent worth and dignity of every person;
2) justice, equity, and compassion in human relations;
3) acceptance of one another and encouragement to spiritual growth in our congregations;
4) a free and responsible search for truth and meaning;
5) the right of conscience and the use of the democratic process within our congregations and in society at large;
6) the goal of world community with peace, liberty, and justice for all; and
7) respect for the interdependent web of all existence of which we are a part.

Respect the inherent worth and dignity of every person. At my church, Paint Branch Unitarian Universalist, this principle is not merely stated but is lived. I have found complete acceptance by members of the church of the experiences I choose to share.

I have lived a full life. I have traveled, had two marriages and two partners, and been blessed with two adult children and two grandchildren. I have been a spiritual seeker all of my life and my image of "God" has changed from a patriarch in the sky to nothingness, creator, Mother Earth, Nature, the Tao, to a field of light and compassion. Until my forties, I sought answers from the world around me, and then with age and (I hope) wisdom, I looked for answers inside.

At 40, I started internally exploring the larger questions again. My partner helped lead me to meditation. She has practiced meditation since her teenage years. At times, particularly when communing with nature, I would sense a stillness inside. I of course grasped at this state, wanting it to continue. It has taken years to let go of judgments, cravings, and aversions, and to focus on feelings in my body. My gateway to meditation and equanimity began with jin shin acupressure and Process Acupressure and grew as I also became immersed in Buddhist psychology.

I started practicing meditation with a large Buddhist community, the Insight Meditation Community of Washington (IMCW),[20] founded by Tara Brach in the late 1990's, and then with two smaller subgroups of the community. The loving-kindness Buddhist meditation group knows my story and has accepted me totally. Tara speaks of learning how to deal with emotions and feelings in the "Coming Home to Your Body" chapter of her book, *Radical Acceptance: Embracing Your Life with the Heart of a Buddha.*[21]

> I simply waited, and in that pause I began to notice the feelings and sensations in my body. The anger felt like a mounting pressure on my chest and throat. My shoulders and hands were tight, my jaw was clenched. I felt my heart pounding, felt the heat in my face. This was horribly uncomfortable…. At these times, we begin to see how interconnected our mind and body are…. Sensations in the body are ground zero, the place where we directly experience the entire play of life…. As I stood there that night…feeling and "letting be" what was happening inside me, the sensations slowly began to shift.

People with mental illness are generally not helped in learning how to deal with their feelings. Psychiatrists prescribe medication to blunt or eliminate feelings. Most psychiatrists see their patients only for fifteen minute sessions to review their medications. My current psychiatrist is atypical in that our talk therapy sessions are fifty minutes and our weekly group sessions are specifically focused on talking about feelings. I believe that to obtain good mental health means that the physical, emotional and spiritual needs also must be addressed.

Community is vital to me, as are individual relationships. I worked to become a part of these groups as a way to maintain my health and well-being. I also worked to develop close relationships with a number of people. If there had been a community or group for me to join that was offered through Washington Adventist or Sheppard Pratt, I believe it would have helped me a great deal in transitioning back to "normalcy." I believe that I was considered to be too functional for their outpatient groups. Montgomery General did offer an outpatient program that I attended, and they also suggested a therapy group. I am still a member of it and am deeply grateful to my doctor and to the group members for the sharing that occurs there. Amidst the chaos I have been given close friends, individually and in groups, who have supported me and held me in their love and light. I cannot thank them enough.

Acupressure, finger pressure on specific acupoints, has helped me learn to be aware of my emotions and where they are held in my body. It helps me to stay centered and grounded when I have been able to receive it or give it to others. I was first exposed to this healing modality in 1993. It was then that I was diagnosed with reflex sympathetic dystrophy in my right foot. I couldn't walk on it and it was painful even to the lightest touch. The circulation was very bad. I had seen an orthopedist, podiatrist, and neurologist, and no one had a way to help me except to send me to a physical therapist. My foot was not improving with the physical therapy treatments, and one day the physical therapist's assistant gave me a business card of someone who did acupressure, Lowell Singe. She suggested I try it and thought that it would help me. I had nothing to lose, so I went to see him.

Five treatments of acupressure once a week and my foot was healed. My logical mind couldn't understand how this could have happened, but I was very thankful for it. I continued to see him and started noticing other things such as how relaxed I was after his treatments and how good I felt. I also remember crying a whole weekend for no logical reason. I believe it was a cathartic release. During his treatments, which are based on the fundamentals of Traditional Chinese Medicine and applying relatively light finger pressure to acupoints (the same points that acupuncturists use), I would sink into a dreamlike state. I was still present and fully aware of my body and all the sensations it was experiencing. These included discomfort, twinges, pain, involuntary movements, twitches, a sense of pins and needles, energy movement. Occasionally I would "see" with my eyes closed images or colors.

A year later, Lowell offered an apprenticeship program of 500 hours to learn how to practice jin shin acupressure. I took the course and practiced on friends and family. The results were amazing. Physical ailments lessened and in some cases disappeared. The biggest shift occurred, however, in how the client perceived their body and health. The link between mind and body and emotions became clearer to the client.

Several years later, Lowell suggested that I take a workshop in Process Acupressure that was being offered by Aminah Raheem,[22] the founder of this work. I did so and found this to be the most profound bodywork I had ever experienced. Process Acupressure is a healing modality that applies finger pressure on Traditional Chinese acupressure points to affect and integrate bodywork with emotional and spiritual processing. Clients are empowered to control the depth of their experience while the practitioner facilitates and provides a safe place for the exploration of cellular memories. During much of my journey since May 2003, I have received acupuncture and acupressure.

In March 2009, I participated in a Process Acupressure session as the client. The last Sunday of each month, several practitioners get together to exchange acupressure. The founder of Process Acupressure developed a series of over 100 protocols for addressing specific physical concerns, including a basic protocol for starting and ending a session. I lay down on a massage table fully clothed with a blanket over me.

Usually there is only one practitioner per client, but in this particular session I had two practitioners. Cindy and Penny were my practitioners. Cindy asked me what my intention was for the session. I responded that I wanted to let go of the fear that I might have skin cancer. The dermatologist took two biopsies from my face the week before. I also asked that I be able to let go of trying to control my mother and allowing her to move from an assisted living center to an independent living situation. My third request was that I notice the beauty of spring around me.

Cindy repeated my intentions, asking that any healing also extend out to others in the world who feel the same emotions. She then asked that my soul or inner wisdom guide the session and that hers and Penny's souls be present to assist mine. I also invited the ocean to be present and any other loving, compassionate, and healing spirits be present. Cindy and Penny then began the protocol of stretching my legs and applying finger pressure to specific points on my back. I noticed that I was sinking into the table, relaxing, and feeling supported.

Cindy encouraged me to continue to relax and to feel the care and support. Cindy invited me to notice what was going on in my body. She asked if there was any discomfort, tightness, or pain. I scanned my body and then shared that my head felt tight with pressure. I noticed a band around my head. Cindy asked me to say more about the band. The first thing that popped into my mind was, "it's not a jazz band." We all laughed. The Universe or soul has quite a sense of humor. I focused on the band again and said that it was thin and made of metal and that the pressure was less.

Cindy and Penny had been touching points on my back and not on my head, but their touch had affected my head. Cindy then asked me if there was any pain in my head, and I replied yes, behind my left eye. She asked me how big it was and I replied that it was about the size of a fist. She asked if it was time to let go of it. I replied, "yes." She then asked if there was anything that this pain could tell me: why it was here, what I needed to know. I asked the pain, and it said, "quit trying to control others, it doesn't work. Here is another f____ing growth opportunity. Every experience I have is exactly what my soul needs to grow." I asked if these growth opportunities could be a little easier. And then I remembered that I am very hardheaded at times, although I am improving. When the hour session was over, I felt so much lighter. There was no dull ache in my head, and my visual sense was clearer. I could see the little buds on the tree out the window and felt very connected to Penny and Cindy. We thanked our souls and healing spirits that had been with us.

THANK YOU RIVER

8/10/03

River teach me how to breathe
Help me let go and float free
Cast off what I don't need
Give my will over to thee
Ever more gracefully
Loosening my grasp
On what is gone and past
Not striving for more
or stroking hard to the shore
Rather let me float here
Carried and held near
Caressed by the flow
Around above and below
I now let go

My family has been very concerned for me and has worried tremendously about me. My son has always been there for me and has worked through hospital and health care systems to help me in the best way possible. He has always acted from a compassionate heart and tried to understand my reality shifts. My former partner has also advised him and has done her best to try to help me. My daughter lived with me when I was living in two realities at the same time and held a space for me to be. My father paid to medically evacuate me from Madagascar. My stepmother came and stayed with me, cleaning, cooking, and providing companionship when I was released from the hospital. She never left my side until I told her I was not taking my medications. Then not realizing how ill I was, she went to get her hair done, and I left on my next manic journey.

No one has berated me for my crazy actions or for disappearing without a word to anyone. I felt at the time that my family and friends would die if I disclosed anything to them. My fear at times told me that those closest to me were already dead. During one psychotic episode, I decided that I was already dead. This life could not be so terrible, so I must have been killed by extraterrestrials. Then I was left here on earth in a continual state of suffering. As I came out of that psychotic episode, I was so thankful to walk outside and smell the air and see the beauty everywhere around me.

My relationship with the Universe has deepened as I have learned not to mistake my psychotic directives for that of the Universe. My understanding of peace has changed from a projection outside of myself to internal peaceful states. I am no longer at war with myself. I meditate each day to notice my thoughts and feelings and any reactivity I have towards a person or situation. My practice is to be mindful, to slow life down and be aware, to stop the busyness. If it took five psychotic episodes for my compassion for other beings to grow this deep, it has been worth it. I do not know if the human species will survive the changes that humankind has placed in motion. I do believe that the way to change consciousness is one heart at a time. I do not know what the future brings, and I try not to live in the past or the future, but the here and now. I am told that my mental health disorder is permanent, and I will probably have to take medications for it the rest of my life. We shall see.

I have shared my journey with you in the hope that it will help you understand one person's experience with a schizo-affective disorder. Perhaps it may also provide ways for you and me to look differently at your or another's mental health. By sharing the pain of this disease I hope that it will illicit compassion. I do not know what the next stages of my life journey might be. I recognize that when I see a homeless person that I could be that person. Mental illnesses can have devastating effects on those who have them and their loved ones. I have been very fortunate. I will work hard to make sure that I am taking good care of all aspects of myself: mental, physical, emotional, and spiritual. Helen Keller said that "Life is a daring adventure". I choose to look at my life that way and trust that life and my illness will be full of learnings for me and increased compassion for me and others.

APPENDIX

From my experience I recommend the following.

When a Loved One Appears to be Mentally Unstable

1. Examine your own feelings and deal with those first.
2. If you can stay in compassion, talk to your loved one and let her know how much you care for her and that you are concerned by things she is saying or doing—be specific. Ask her to explain why she is saying or doing those things and really listen.
3. Ask what she is feeling and really listen.
4. One of the best things you can give him is a feeling that he is not alone and that you love him and want to help him in the best way possible.
5. Acknowledge that his perceptions may be in a very heightened state and that he may be experiencing another reality.
6. Ask him what he believes. What is the belief that underlies the emotions or behavior. Don't argue about the belief but understand how the behavior or emotions are controlled by the beliefs. Usually there will be a belief system that stems from a true piece of information but has spiraled into a cadre of beliefs that are not "real" in everyday reality.
7. As strange as beliefs may seem, they are very real to the person, and the person is probably very scared and confused by them. Your reassurance that you are there for them and will stand by them and help them in the best way you know how helps to sustain the relationship.
8. Seek professional advice, but don't discount your loved one's feelings or what she says. Professionals are not always right!

A Guide to Help Me and Others: Signs of Losing It

12/16/06; Revised 4/5/07

The following are my precursors to psychotic episodes.

More depression, unwillingness or unable to get out of bed

Lack of sleep—not able to sleep, not feeling tired, becoming manic

Thinking that personalized signs are all around me—red stoplights, license plates

Stopping meditation

Not paying attention to personal appearance

Wearing the same clothes

Becoming more isolated

Not leaving the house, or determination to leave the house and area

Not connecting with other people—very little talking or expressing what is happening with me

Hearing frequencies of sound, especially at night, that keep me awake

Hypersensitivity in sensory experience

Blindfolding myself or cutting off my vision in some way

Limiting sensory stimuli—no music

Seeing patterns on the wall (jail bars)

The week after a lot of stress

Beliefs that are strong and unquestionable and are not based on observable facts (water, radiation, algae)

Leaving notes warning people of the beliefs—water, radiation, etc.

Feeling like I am being directed to do what I do; may precede personalized signs

Believing that I am being pursued, under surveillance

Unable to be the observer of my thoughts or beliefs, no distance from them

Seeing lights flashing

Moving head up and down voluntarily to control thoughts and frequencies

Vacant look in my eyes, like no one is home

Not answering questions

Not returning a loved one's telephone calls

Intuition, attaching special significance to things

Sense of personal mission

Things make sense internally, but it's risky to share them with others—too complex, convoluted, and therefore difficult to get a reality check

Worry about the water—drinking and bathing

Compulsive spending

Stopping medication

Why I Stopped Taking Medications

1. I did not realize that I had a mental illness. I believed that my thoughts were true and accurate.
2. The medications are expensive: on Medicare with American Association of Retired Persons (AARP) supplemental coverage, 90 days' worth of three medications cost approximately $600 in my co-pay.
3. The medications did not seem to make any difference in my thoughts and actions.
4. I felt good and that I no longer needed medication.
5. The side effects are profound: a proclivity for diabetes and tardive dyskenesia, lack of feelings, numbness in my hands and arms, dry mouth, weight gain, hair loss, and decline in sexual libido.
6. The medications made me act like a drugged zombie, unable to leave my bed.
7. The medications made me require at least ten hours of sleep each night with a nap in the afternoon.

Résumé

LYNN JOHNSON, MA, LMT, Dipl. ABT
Organizational Consultant
Group Trainer and Facilitator
Licensed Massage Therapist
Diplomate Asian Bodywork Therapist
Certified Process Acupressure Therapist

Lynn is Co-Founder of New Visions Consulting. This organization helps leaders make good, effective, quick decisions by learning to better balance and integrate the essential information and wisdom that comes from emotions, intuition, body and mind. This learning enhances individual, group and organizational effectiveness, decision-making and performance. **Lynn is a dynamic leader who:**

- **brings over 30 years of experience in facilitating individual and organizational awareness and change.** Since 1995 she has had one foot in the world of training, senior management and business and the other in integrative medicine. She sees patterns and interrelationships, helps to define and resolve problems, and initiates and guides change. Lynn structures opportunities for deepening awareness, developing perceptual, cognitive, intuitive, and affective skills, and aligning values with actions. This enables individuals and groups to gain clarity on what is really happening and to make more effective choices.

- **imparts a larger vision and builds on the strengths of others to achieve short- and long-term goals and objectives.** She has twenty years of experience in management. For eight years, she managed the day-to-day operations of the National Academy of Sciences' (NAS) Office of Contracts and Grants. She oversaw a staff of 32 and the fiscal management of $760M in contracts and grants.

- **improves the productivity of work groups and organizational profitability through training and by facilitating the**

interaction of teams. As Training Coordinator for the Office of the Chief Financial Officer, she created and presented training sessions and half-day leadership modules for the NAS.

- **co-authored the book,** *Reinventing the University,* **and has written and published over 15 chapters, articles and papers on communication, adult learning and learning organizations**.
- **lived and worked on three continents with diverse groups** ranging from subsistence farmers and Bedouins to university faculty, government administrators and business owners. She now combines her research and study of adult learning and effective communication with fundamentals of energy, new physics and Chinese medicine.

Communication and adult learning are common threads that weave through her varied careers. She is a change agent who models integrative wisdom and energetic alignment to facilitate learning in groups and individuals. She believes that healthy people and vibrant, profitable organizations grow from balanced centers of interconnected relationships with a sense of purpose.

EMPLOYMENT HISTORY

1995–2003	**Practitioner of Acupressure,** The Spectrum Center for Natural Medicine, LLC, Silver Spring, MD
2003	**Co-Founder**, New Visions Consulting, Silver Spring, MD.
2002–2003	**Co-Owner,** The Spectrum Center for Natural Medicine, LLC.
2001–2002	**Training Coordinator,** Office of the Chief Financial Officer, The National Academies, Washington, DC
2000–2001	**Associate Director,** Office of Contracts and Grants, Post Award Administration, The National Academies, Washington, DC
1994–2000	**Manager,** Private Sector, The National Academies, Washington, DC
1988–1994	**Director,** Office of Research Administration,

	Towson State University, Towson, MD
1986–1988	**Assistant to the Director,** Office of Grants and Contracts, New Mexico State University, Las Cruces, New Mexico
1985	**Women in Development Fellow,** Master's research, Honduras, Central America
1982–1984	**Staff Assistant,** Honduras Agricultural Research Project, New Mexico State University, Las Cruces, New Mexico
1980–1982	**Head,** Television and Audio-Visual Center, King Faisal University, Al Hassa, Saudi Arabia
1979	**Head,** Television Section, Loughborough University of Technology, Loughborough, United Kingdom
1976–1978	**Peace Corps Volunteer** - Technical Advisor, Ministry of Education and Ministry of Agriculture, El Salvador, Central America
1974–1975	**Associate Director/Operations Director,** NBC-WRC-TV, DC.
1972–1974	**Producer/Director,** WNVT-TV, Annandale, Virginia
1971–1973	**Para-Legal Specialist/Consultant,** Communications Law Firm, Washington, DC
1970	**Assistant to the Special Projects Director,** WGHP-TV, NC

EDUCATIONAL BACKGROUND

2007	Licensed as a Certified Massage Therapist and Diplomate of Asian Bodywork Therapy
2000	Certified as a Process Acupressure practitioner
1986	M.A., Interdisciplinary (International Communications), New Mexico State, 4.0
1970	B.A., Radio, TV & Motion Pictures, University of North Carolina, Chapel Hill

LANGUAGES

Spanish: Foreign Service Institute rating 3, fluent speaking, good reading ability.

Endnotes

1 According to DSM IV, American Psychiatric Association, 1994, "schizo-affective is a disturbance in which a mood episode and the active-phase symptoms of Schizophrenia occur together and were preceded or are followed by at least two weeks of delusions or hallucinations without prominent mood symptoms."

2 See www.psychiatryonline.com.

3 A simplified description of depression, bipolar, paranoid schizophrenia, and schizo-affective disorder can be found at www.allpsych.com.

4 Dennison, Paul and Gail E. (1989). *Brain Gym*. Ventura, CA: Educational Kinesiology Foundation.

5 Tolle, Eckhart. (2005). *A New Earth: Awakening to Your Life's Purpose*. New York: Plume, Penguin Group.

6 Sinnott, Jan & Johnson, Lynn. (1996). *Reinventing the University: A Radical Proposal for a Problem-Focused University*. Norwood, NJ: Ablex Publishing Corp.

7 Tolle, Eckhart. (1999). *Power of Now: A Guide to Spiritual Enlightenment* (p. 38, hardcover; p. 46, paperback). Novato, CA: New World Publishing.

8 Acupressure is a form of healing touch developed in China several thousand years ago. See www.SoulLightening.com.

9 See www.ShamanicSpring.com and www.SandraIngerman.com for additional information about shamanism.

10 Developed by John Friend. "Anusara" means "flowing with grace" and is one of the most therapeutically effective and spiritually inspiring form of Hatha yoga. See www.yogalifestyle.com/CDANJFAnusaraYogaEssentials.htm.

11 Hatha yoga is a holistic system of breathing exercises and postures that balance the mind, body, and spirit.

12 Acupuncture is used in Traditional Chinese Medicine (TCM) to free the flow of energy throughout the body.

13 Jin Shin Jytsu was developed in Japan and is based on the same acupressure points as acupuncture but without needles.

14 See www.SoulLighteningAcupressure.com.

15 Shiatsu is a form of bodywork that stimulates acupressure points and involves more rhythmic compression and stretches. See www.altmedicine.about.com/od/massage/a/shiatsu.htm.

16 Tolle, Eckhart. (1999). *The Power of Now: A Guide to Spiritual Enlightenment*. Novato, CA: New World Library.

17 Bipolar disorder with psychotic episodes is defined in DSM-IV.

18 Tolle, Eckhart. (2006). *A New Earth: Awakening to Your Life's Purpose* (p. 119). New York: Penguin Group Inc.

19 Costain, Thomas B. (2006). *Silver Chalice*. Chicago: Loyola Press.

20 For information on IMCW and Tara Brach, see www.imcw.org.

21 Brach, Tara. (2003). *Radical Acceptance: Embracing Your Life with the Heart of a Buddha*. New York, NY: Bantam Books. p. 95.

22 For information on Aminah Raheem, see www.soullightening.com.